A *Golden Hands* PATTERN BOOK
MACRAMÉ

RANDOM HOUSE   NEW YORK

Library of Congress Cataloging in Publication Data
Main entry under title:
Macramé: a Golden hands pattern book.
"A Golden hands book."
"Part of this material was published . . . in Golden
hands [and] Golden hands monthly."
First published in 1973 under title: The Golden hands
book of macramé.
1. Macramé—Patterns.   I. Golden hands.
TT840.G6 1974   746.4   73-20577
ISBN 0-394-49073-8

Manufactured in the United States of America
First American Edition

Macramé supplies are available from the following addresses:

Atlas Handicrafts Ltd., P.O. Box 27, Laurel Street, Preston
PR1 3XS, England. Mail orders are accepted and a catalogue
is available. Craft yarns of Rhode Island, 603 Mineral
Springs Avenue, P.O. Box 385, Pawtucket, R.I. 02862.
F. J. Fawcett, 129 South Street, Boston, Massachusetts
02111. J. E. Frick Company, 40 North Front Street,
Philadelphia, Pennsylvania 19106. Lily Mills Company,
Shelby, North Carolina 28150. Macramé and Weaving
Supply Company, 63 East Adams Street, Chicago, Illinois
60603.

Lampshade frames available from:
Atlas Handicrafts Ltd., P.O. Box 27, Laurel Street, Preston
PR1 3XS, England. Oriental Lamp & Shade Company, 810
Lexington Avenue, New York, New York 10021.

EDITOR: Marigold Popplewell

MACRAMÉ CONSULTANT: Kit Pyman

AUTHENTICATOR: Ena Milton

PHOTOGRAPHERS
Michael Murray, Malcolm Aird, John Carter,
Roger Charity, Richard Clapp, Phillip Gallard, Chris Lewis,
Peter Rand, Peter Watkins.

ILLUSTRATORS
Paul Williams, Barbara Firth, Faulkner Marks.

DESIGNERS
Mavis Bee, Germaine Brotherton, Jennifer Cordell,
Marjorie Craske, Audrey Hersch, Lilian Hughes,
Kit Pyman, Lilian Temple, Hilary Turnbull.

We would like to thank the following for their help and
co-operation: Atlas Handicrafts Ltd, English Sewing Ltd,
John Lewis, Patons and Baldwins Ltd, Peter Robinson,
Serpentine Restaurant, Hyde Park, Timex Corporation.

About this book . . .

For those who are wondering what macramé actually is, it can be defined simply as the art of knotting. It originated in the middle east and has been popular spasmodically over the years, including in Victorian times when it became very fashionable.

Today, we bring you the Golden Hands Book of Macramé with 50 items to make, all illustrated in color and with easy-to-follow instructions. The wide variety of patterns range from fashion accessories, such as dress and pants suit trimmings, Cavandoli watchbands for all the family, a hat and a little girl's jumper, to home furnishings such as window and wall hangings, lampshades, pillows and a suede hassock – the list is endless.

Do not be deterred if you are a beginner. Learn how to do macramé from the Crash Course at the back of the book. The course describes all the basic techniques involved and each one is illustrated with a diagram. It couldn't be simpler! All you need to practice is a working board, string, a pair of hands and you'll be starting your favorite pattern the very next day.

Creating your own designs in macramé is a way of imprinting your own personality on the work and can be rewarding, but if you are frightened of embarking on this right away, why not try adapting some of these patterns to suit your own particular needs? Add a fringe to a valance, cover an old doorstop, or brighten your clothes with macramé cuffs and edgings.

Whatever you thought about macramé before, we think you will soon agree that it is both an easy and enjoyable way of beautifying your home and enlarging your wardrobe.

CONTENTS

50 Designs for the Family and Home

Great beaded trimming in macramé. Make it in any color to match your favorite dress or add a touch of glamor to a long evening outfit.

2

A must for the fashion conscious child, this lovely shawl has been made in rug yarn so that it is soft and comfortable to wear.

 3

A smart and practical vest for every day. Easy to make, easy to keep clean.

4 *Cheap and easy to make, this vest combines the effects of macramé and suede. Wear it over a bright shirt or sweater to show off its natural coloring.*

5 *The beautiful bag also combines the effects of macramé and suede. It contains many different knots and will provide a source of inspiration to anyone interested in the craft.*

7

The stunning vest is made in rayon cord or rattail for a soft, silky finish. Wear it on its own if you dare, but if not, an open-neck shirt would look just as good.

6

This chunky necklace with blue ceramic beads is made with the basic macramé knots. It would make the perfect gift for any of your friends or for yourself!

8

A simple motif is repeated to make this unusual and attractive necklace. Make it in an evening.

9 This headscarf will not be blown off in the wind! There are two ties, one behind the neck and one under the chin. The scarf is made almost entirely with alternating square knots so is much easier to make than it looks.

10

A smart bag to wear with any outfit. It is made in Persian pattern and decorated at the top with picots.

11

These handsome Cavandoli watchbands made in three sizes to fit a man, woman and child, are both practical and eye-catching. They can be worn for everyday or for special occasions.

12

Switch on to summer in this great macramé hat! It is made with raffene, and believe it or not, bell wire; so why not make the most unusual hat of the season.

13

This matching sash and headband are the perfect accessories for the simple outfit. The sash is adjustable for any size hip and the tassels can be as long or as short as you want.

14

*Half an hour to spare?
Then, why not make this
simple choker and wear it
in the same evening.*

15

*The inexpensive way to
look beautiful. This
beaded jacket is made
with cotton yarn. Buy a
paper pattern as a guide
and make it in your own
size.*

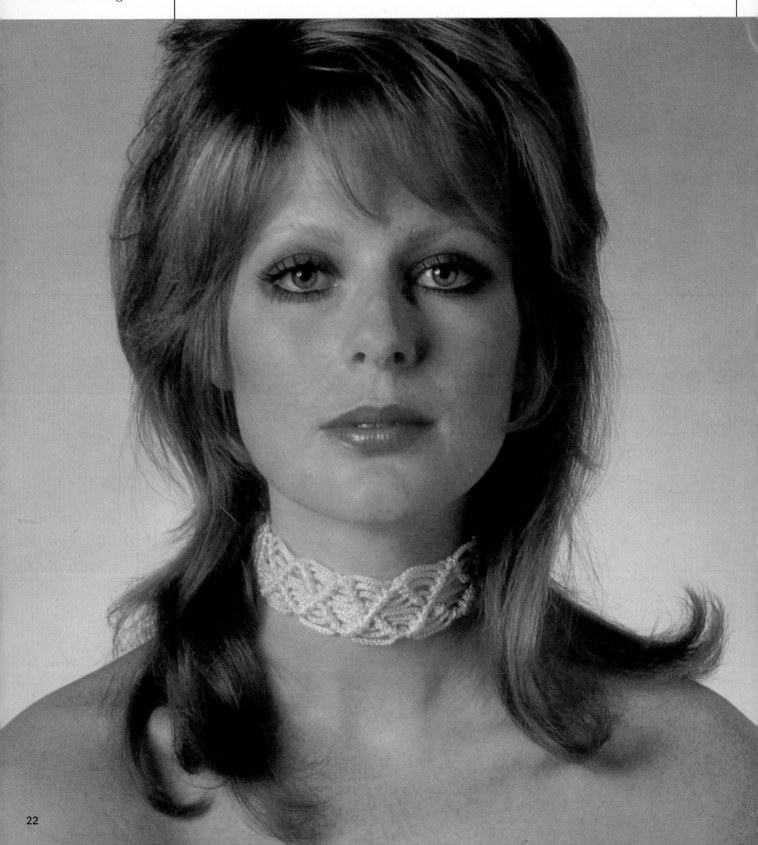

16

Make this belt and bracelet in different colors to match your favorite outfit. You can choose any buckle to fit in with the color scheme.

17

A deep macramé fringe transforms a simple shawl into something really special. The shawl is shaped so that it will not slide off the shoulders and takes only one yard of material.

18

A bracelet in leather for the man in your life. Made with square knots, it is quick and easy to make.

19

This sweet little jumper has been made almost entirely with double half hitches and alternating square knots. It would make a darling outfit for a party or for a special day out.

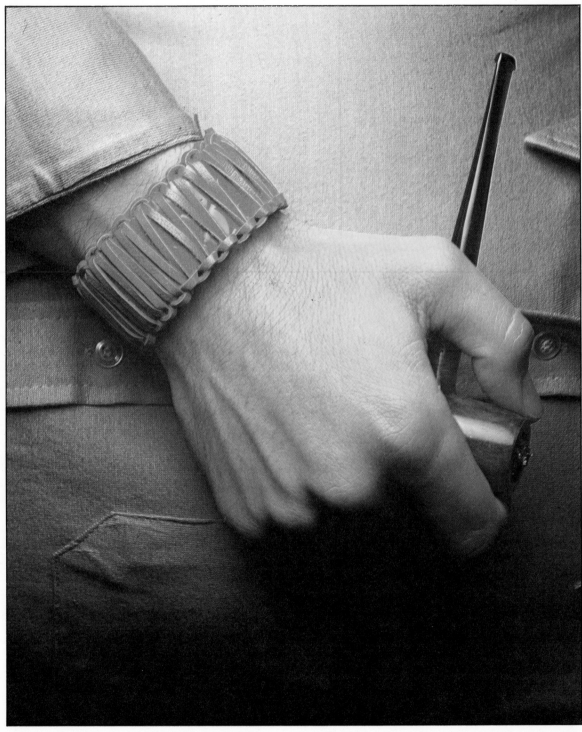

20/21

Make these macramé panels and cuffs and add a touch of sophistication to your pants suits, old or new. Finish off the effect with the matching necklace or make it separately as an accessory to any outfit in your wardrobe.

22

An elegant bag made with double half hitches: just the thing for those special evenings out.

23

The luxury of lurex can be yours if you make this matching belt and bracelet. Worn with a dark fabric, the effect will be particularly stunning.

Instructions for designs 1-24

1 Dress trimming

You will need
Nylon cord, 120 yds per repeat
7 med. beads (2 for every 2in repeat on trimming)

How to make the hem trimming
Cut 5 lengths for every repeat, each 24 inches.
*Make one knotted 3-loop picot. Using 3rd thread from left, DHH diagonally to the left. Double the 4th thread and pin to the working surface just above the leader (see diagram a). DHH over leader.

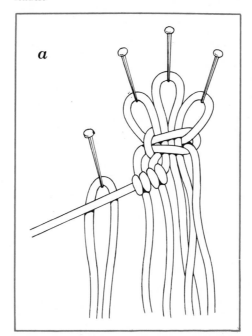

a

Using 5th thread from the left, DHH diagonally to the left with all threads except previous leader. Using 6th thread from the left as leader, DHH diagonally to the right. Introducing 5th thread as before, complete to correspond with first half. Pass 2 center threads through a bead*. Position another 3-loop picot 2 inches along working surface from first picot. Repeat from * to *.
Using 10th thread from left as leader, DHH diagonally to the right over next 5 threads. Using 9th thread from left as leader, DHH diagonally to the right over next 6 threads. Using 9th thread from left as leader, DHH diagonally to the left over the next 3 threads. Using 10th thread from the left as leader, DHH diagonally to the left over next 4 threads. Repeat from * to * with another 5 threads, again positioning picot 2 inches from previous picot.
Pass 10th and 11th threads from the left through a bead. Knot 12th threads around the 9th, 10th and 11th thread directly under the bead to secure, thus forming a collecting knot.
Using the center 2 threads at point of motif, DHH over left once. Knot the outside right threads of this group around other 5 threads. Continue in this way and finally join the last motif to the first. Sew picots and top edge of trimming to garment.

How to make the neck trimming
Measure length of trimming required, cut thread twice this length plus 8 inches. Cut a 2nd cord 8 times the length of the first cord plus 8 inches. Double the first length and thread on 5 beads for every 4 inches of trimming required. Tie a loose overhand knot to hold beads on cord.
Position 2 loops together on working surface, the doubled length holding the beads placed inside the 2nd doubled length. 2 inches from the pin, make a square knot with the outer threads and

using the center threads as a core. Make a 2nd square knot ½ inch below the first, push up to first knot to form picots, (see diagram b). Position one bead below the last knot worked.

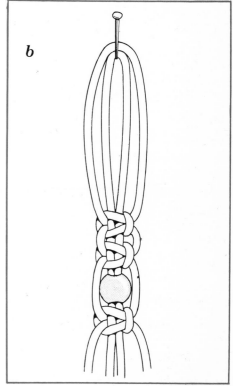

b

Continue in this way for length required alternating 2 square knots with picots with a bead, taking outer thread around outside of beads, and ending with square knots. Turn under threads at each end and slip stitch in place. Slip stitch braid to garment.

Collecting knot worked over two threads

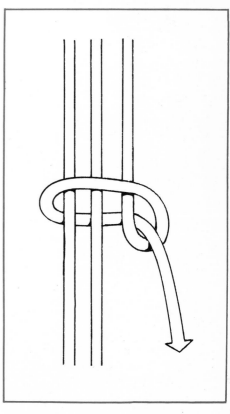

24

If you're always forgetting your bag, leaving it on trains, then this is the bag for you! Fashionable and easy to make, try making it in two tones to match any of your clothes.

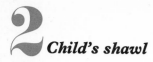

2 Child's shawl

You will need
4 4 oz. skeins of soft rug wool

Measurements
Width, 30in
Depth, 15in
Fringe, 8in

How to make the shawl
Cut a foundation thread 36 inches and pin onto working surface. Cut and attach threads as follows: 3 lengths each 48 inches, one length 144 inches, 3 lengths each 48 inches, 14 lengths each 96 inches, 30 lengths each 120 inches, 14 lengths each 96 inches, 3 lengths each 48 inches, one length 144 inches, 3 lengths each 48 inches. Cut a separate thread 36 inches and using it as a leader knot one row of horizontal DHHs. Divide threads into groups of 14. Take the 2 center threads of each group and using them as leaders DHH diagonally to left and right with the adjacent threads. Take the 6 center threads and using them as a core make one square knot with the pair of threads on either side. Complete the diamond shape by knotting DHHs over leaders from adjacent diamonds. Leaving out the 7 threads on either side of the shawl, take the center left thread of each diamond and weave it under and over the right hand threads of each diamond. Continue in this way with all the left hand threads of each diamond. (The diamonds containing the weaving should fall underneath and between the diamonds containing the square knots.) Then, using the outside threads on each side of each group as leaders, DHH diagonally inward to a point, to form the base of the diamond. Continue in this way for another 7 rows, leaving out 7 threads on either side of each row so that the work forms a triangle.

To finish
Make an overhand knot on each pair of threads, trim to 8 inches and sew in foundation thread and attached cords.

3 Vest

You will need
4 2oz balls white medium weight knitting wool
4 2oz balls contrasting medium weight knitting wool
Medium sized crochet hook
Darning needle
Stiff paper marked out in one-inch squares

Measurements
To fit 36–38in bust
Length at center back, 19in excluding fringe

How to make the vest
Transfer pattern outline to paper marked in one-inch squares and pin to working surface (see graph pattern).
Using contrasting yarn, crochet a chain to fit up left front edge, across neck and shoulder, around armhole, across back shoulder, neck and shoulder, around armhole and across shoulder, neck and down right front. Pin chain around outline at one-inch intervals.
Cut 56 lengths each 216 inches, 14 lengths each 154 inches, 2 lengths each 110 inches and 2 lengths each 81 inches, all white; cut 55 lengths each 216 inches, 14 lengths each 154 inches, 4 lengths each 110 inches and 2 lengths each 81 inches, all in the contrasting color. Attach threads through crochet chain, using crochet hook. Fold the 4 110 inch lengths of contrasting yarn, so that one end measures 4 inches and the other end measures 106 inches. Hook these lengths into the crochet chain at the 2 front neck corners and at the armhole end of each front shoulder. Fold the 2 110 inch lengths white, in the same way and hook into the crochet chain at the armhole ends of the back shoulders. Darn all short ends into the crochet chain and trim. Alternating the colors, attach the 216 inch lengths doubled as follows: 8 lengths of each color onto front neck section; 18 white and 17 contrasting lengths onto the back neck section; 6 white and 5 contrasting lengths onto each front shoulder section; 5 white and 6 contrasting lengths onto each back shoulder section.

Yoke
Beginning at the highest point of each shoulder, make rows of alternating square knots, alternating the color of the outer threads of each knot on each row, so that the work forms into horizontal stripes. On every alternated row, hook the 2 extra edge threads at each side through the crochet chain. Continue until the curve of the armhole is reached.

Underarm
Fold the 81 inch lengths so that one end measures 4 inches and the other 77 inches. Hook one length of the contrasting color into each front of underarm and one white length into each back of underarm. Darn in ends as before.
Attach 154 inch lengths doubled and following the color sequence attach 7 white lengths and 7 contrasting lengths onto each underarm section. Continue row of alternated square knots as before until work measures 10 inches from shoulder, ending with a row of white square knots.
On each group of 4 threads make 5 square knots, using white threads as cores. Make one row of white square knots. Make another braid of 5 contrasting color square knots on each group. At each of left and right front edges make a single knotted chain 13 times with the outer 2 threads. On each alternate group of 4 threads make 8 white square knots. On every other alternate group of 4 threads make 9 white square knots. Using contrasting color threads from each braid of 8 square knots as leaders, DHH diagonally out to right and left across next 3 threads on each side.

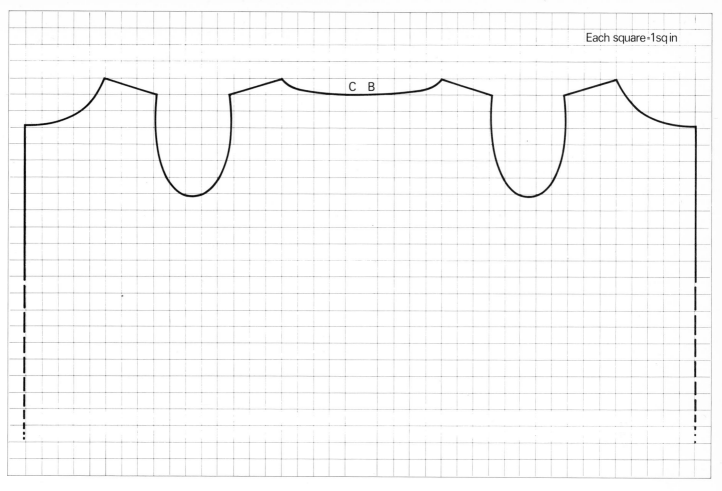

C B

Each square=1sq in

Graph pattern for outline of vest

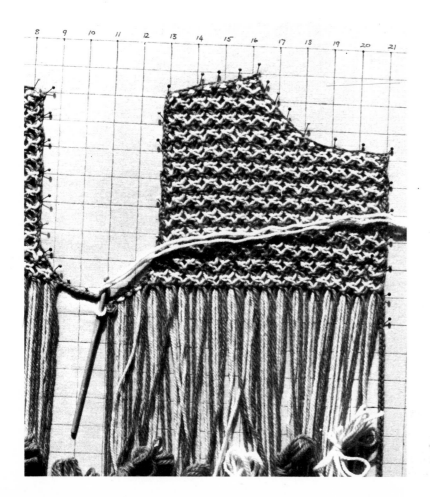

On each group of 4 contrasting color threads make one square knot. On each group of 4 white threads make 3 square knots. Using same contrasting color leaders as before, DHH back across 3 threads to form a core. Hook 2 outer threads at each end through crochet chain. Make 2nd half of braids pattern to correspond in reverse with the first half. Complete vest with striped rows of alternating square knots until center back measures 18 inches.
Make 2 rows of alternated overhand knots and trim fringe to about 4 inches.

To finish
Join shoulder seams and press work very lightly under a damp cloth, using a warm iron.

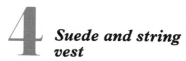

4 Suede and string vest

You will need
2¼ lbs cotton string medium thickness
Piece of suede or leather 10½in x 15in
68 round wooden beads
Leather puncher

Measurements
To fit 34in to 38in bust
Length from shoulder to end of fringe 31½in

The vest in the process of being worked

How to make the vest
Front

Punch 64 holes evenly spaced along the 15 inch edge of suede ¼ inch in from the edge. Cut 31 lengths of string 172 inches and one length 206 inches. Double each of the 172 inch lengths and attach onto the suede starting from the right. Divide the 206 inch length so that the right thread is 86 inches and the left thread 120 inches. Attach this longer length on the extreme left and using it as a leader; knot one row of horizontal DHHs. Numbering the threads from one to 64, make 9 square knots on 1.2.3.4., 15.16.17.18., 29.30.31.32., 33.34.35.36., 47.48.49.50., 61.62.63.64.

*Using the 5th of the threads not yet knotted, make one row of diagonal DHHs to the left and using the 6th knot a row of diagonal DHHs to the right. Using the 4th and 7th threads respectively as leaders, knot 2 more rows of diagonal DHHs directly underneath the first rows.

Using the extreme left threads of the same group, as leaders knot a row of diagonal DHHs into the center so that a diamond shape is formed. Make another row of diagonal DHH directly underneath the rows just knotted.*

Repeat from * to * in each of the spaces between the square knots already worked. Leaving threads 1.2., and 63.64., make 3 square knots on the next 4 threads on each side. Taking the next 6 threads in from the right use the center 2 as a core and make 5 square knots. Repeat this with the 6 threads at the base of each of the other 3 diamonds. With the remaining threads make 7 square knots using 2 core threads and one working thread on either side. With the first and last 4 threads make 3 square knots. Using the first thread as a leader knot one row of horizontal DHH's.

[1]Divide all the threads into groups of 4 and make the first half of a square knot 16 times to make a spiral.

Leaving the outer 2 threads on each side make 3 square knots with 15 remaining groups of threads. Using all the threads make 3 square knots on each alternated group. Repeat from ** to **.

Divide the threads into groups of 4 and make 8 square knots on each group.[1] Leaving the outside 2 threads on each side, make the first half of a square knot 10 times on the next 2 groups of 4 threads at each side and alternate group after that, so that 6 groups of 4 threads remain.

***With these remaining groups make one square knot. Then, thread a bead onto each of the

Back of the vest

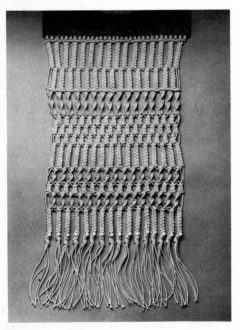

working cords. Repeat both these stages once again. Secure beads with one square knot.***

Divide the threads into groups of 4 and work 3 square knots on each. Leaving the 2 outside threads at each side, make the first half of a square knot 10 times on the next 5 groups of 4 threads on each side and each alternate one after that, so that 3 groups of 4 threads remain. With the remaining threads repeat from *** to ***.

[2]Make 8 square knots onto the 16 groups of 4 threads and then thread a bead onto one of the core threads. Make one square knot to secure. Make an overhand knot at the base of each square knot. Cut ends to measure 6½ inches.[2]

Back (see photograph)

Repeat as for the front until you have knotted one row of horizontal DHHs. Divide the threads into groups of 4 and make 9 square knots on each group. Leaving the 2 outer threads on each side work 7 square knots on the remaining 15 groups of 4 threads. Using the first thread on the left as a leader, knot one row of horizontal DHH. Knot from [1] to [1] in front pattern.

Leaving the 2 outer threads on each side make the first half of a square knot 10 times with the remaining 15 groups of 4 threads. Using all the threads make 3 square knots with each group of 4 threads. Repeat from * to *. Repeat from [2] to [2] in front pattern.

Side tie

Cut 2 lengths each 84 inches and lay them side by side. Secure one and twist the other end clockwise until it is very tight. Double the threads and twist counter-clockwise. Make an overhand knot 4 inches from each end and cut ends. Make a 2nd tie in the same way. Tie in the cords at the waist so that the vest is secure.

Suede neck section

This should be cut out as required, making sure not to cut the neck too large.

5 Shoulder bag

You will need

1lb fine Seine twine or 10/5 linen
One piece string-colored suede 24in by 11½in
2 pieces stiff leather each 9in by ¼in

Measurements

Width, 8in
Depth, 1½in
Length, 10in, excluding fringe
Shoulder strap, 50in from base of bag

How to make the bag

Cut 48 lengths, each 100 inches, two lengths each 64 inches and 14 lengths, each 215 inches. Attach 24 of the 100 inch lengths to one of the 9 inch strips of leather and divide into 4 groups as follows: one group of 4 doubled threads from the left-hand edge to one inch along, leave a ½ inch space, place the 2nd group from 1½ inches along for 2 inches and with 8 doubled threads, leave a ½ inch space, place another group of 8 doubled threads across 2 inches, leave a ½ inch space and place the last group of 4 doubled threads on last inch. Pin the groups in place.

To fill the gaps between the knots, use one of the 64 inch lengths and starting 4 inches from one end of the thread, make one vertical DHH knot between the knots (see diagram a) one between each of the 4 knots in the first group, and so on, carrying the thread across the top of the ½ inch spaces. At the end of the row bring the thread around to below the attached knots and use as leader for one row of horizontal DHHs across all threads.

Using the 2 threads on either side of each space,

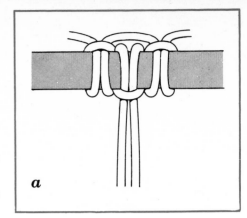

a

make one Chinese crown knot.
Using the 4 threads as leaders, knot 2 rows diagonal DHHs to right and left, starting ½ inch below the Chinese crown knot.

Chinese crown knot

Using these 4 inner threads from each set of DHH, make a Josephine knot one inch below the Chinese crown knot. Using the leaders from the DHHs, make Chinese crown knots alternated with the previous Chinese crown knots even with the Josephine knots and using the outer pairs of threads of the work to make an overhand knot at the same level.

Josephine knot

Turk's head for button

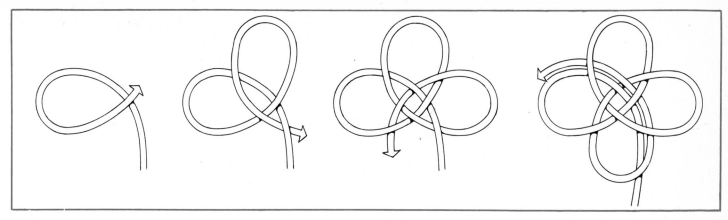

Turk's head for tassel

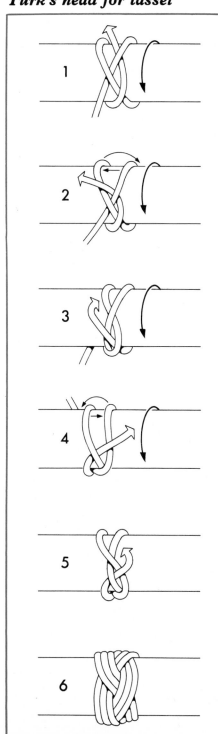

Graph pattern for bag lining

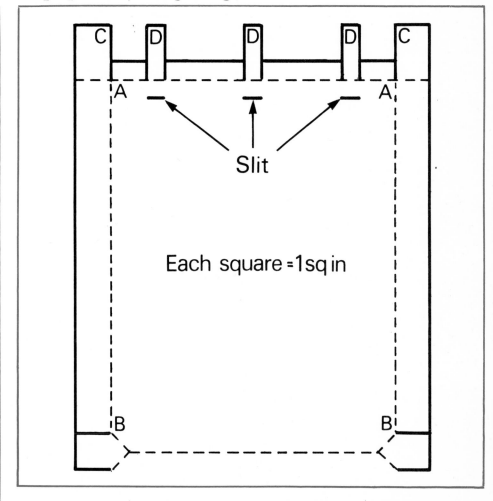

C   D   D   D   C

A   A

Slit

Each square = 1 sq in

B   B

Using the threads from the Chinese crown knots as leaders, DHH diagonally to right and left to form a diamond shape around the Josephine knots. Continue in this way until there are 5 alternated rows of Josephine knots in all, ending with a row of Chinese crown knots. On the rows with 2 Josephine knots, use the 4 outer threads at each side to make an overhand knot even with the Josephine knots. Make a second side for the bag in the same way. For the shoulder strap, use the 14 lengths of 215 inches and work from the middle of the threads towards each end in turn.

Knot diamonds of double diagonal DHH with a 4 strand overhand knot in the center of each and lining the leaders by twisting one over the other. 2 diamonds equal 3 inches. There are 31 diamonds in all in the strap.

Knot 8 diamonds from the center diamond. Link the center side edges of the next diamond with the top of the bag pieces to form a gusset. Link the side edges between the 10th and 11th diamonds with the overhand knot on the bag pieces and continue linking the strap to the bag in this way down the sides. After the last diamond, use the 2 outer threads together with the 2 outer threads of the bag to make a Chinese crown knot even with the last row of Chinese crown knots on the bag. Repeat from the center of the strap down the other side. To make the lower fringe, take the centre 8 threads from the front of the bag together with the centre 8 threads from the back piece and tie with a constrictor knot (see page 88) one inch below the Chinese crown knots.

Cut one length 20 inches and work around the tassel in a Turk's head following the 6 stages illustrated in the diagram.

Once the Turk's head is complete, thread the end into the fringe and trim to about 4½ inches.

Work in the same way on each of the 2 groups of 8 threads on either side of the center group. The remaining 22 threads at each side are taken as one group.

To finish
To make the lining, cut the suede as shown in the graph pattern. Dotted lines make fold lines and S is slit.
Fold the piece in half width-wise, fold the side sections toward each other and glue one on top of the other to make a double thickness gusset. Glue the small flaps at top and bottom of the gussets. Insert lining in bag and position horizontal DHH directly above slits. Turn allowance above fold line between bag and lining and glue in place. Take the strips over the ½ inch spaces between the knots at the top of the bag under the DHH leader and push through slots. Glue strips to inside of bag. Make a Turk's head without a core to make the button fastening and attach it to the center Chinese crown knot at the top of the front of the bag. Attach 3 doubled threads each about 24 inches long to the horizontal DHH leader at the center space on the back of the bag. Divide into 2 groups of 3 threads each and braid each group for 3 inches. Link the two groups with a Turk's head to form a button loop.

6 Necklace with ceramic beads

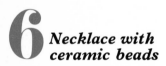

You will need
One 4oz ball white twine
5 large blue ceramic beads
100 small blue glass beads
Scissors
Glue
Tape measure

Measurements
Circumference of necklace, about 16in
Length of center motif, about 8in

How to make the necklace
Cut 2 lengths each 96 inches and 2 lengths each 36 inches. Find the center of the 2 36 inch lengths and of one of the 96 inch lengths. Placing the centers of the 3 lengths together, make an overhand knot 3 inches to the right of the center, and another 3 inches to the left. These 3 threads form the foundation thread. Pin them to the working surface.
Cut 12 lengths each 48 inches and 10 lengths each 84 inches. Taking each thread separately, double it and attach to the foundation thread in the following order: 6 48 inch lengths, 10 84 inch lengths, and 6 48 inch lengths. These should fit comfortably between the 2 knots on the foundation thread. Take the remaining 96 inch length, center it on the work and make a knot 3 inches to the right of the center and pin it beside the knot on the foundation thread. Using this thread as a leader, DHH horizontally across all hanging threads to the left. Make another knot and pin this to the left-hand knot on the foundation thread.
Center motif
This is made with the 10 doubled 84 inch lengths. Pass the 2 center threads through a small bead, then, taking the left-hand thread of these 2 and using it as a leader, DHH diagonally to the left over the remaining 9 threads. In the same way DHH diagonally to the right with the right-hand center thread.
Pass 2 center threads through a small bead and

make a square knot with 4 threads. Using the next thread on either side as a leader, DHH diagonally to left and right, threading a small bead onto the next and each alternate knotting cord (3 beads each side).
Pass the center 2 threads through a small bead. Make a square knot in the center with 8 threads, pass the center 4 threads through a large bead and make another square knot with 8 threads, pass center 2 threads through a small bead and make a square knot with 4 threads.
Make a square knot with the group of 4 threads on each side of the large bead.
Using outside threads as leader, DHH diagonally into the center.
Using outside threads as a leader, DHH diagonally into the center, threading a small bead on next and alternate knotting cords (4 beads each side). Pass center 2 threads through a small bead and make a firm square knot with 4 threads. This draws the motif into a convex shape. Pass center 2 threads through a large bead and make a square knot with 4 threads.
Draw all 7 threads on left side towards large bead and DHH to the right with 8th thread. Repeat on right. Gather all threads together in an overhand knot. Leave 4 inches, pass each thread through a small bead, make an overhand knot, cut near the knot and secure with a little glue.
Side motifs
The motifs on either side are both the same, each using the group of 6 doubled 48 inch lengths.
Pass center 2 threads through a small bead, DHH to left and right over 5 threads. Make a square knot with 8 threads. Pass center 2 threads through a large bead, make a square knot with 8 threads. Pass center 2 threads through a small bead, make a square knot with 4 threads.
Thread 3 beads on the outside leaders and DHH them into the center. Pass the center 2 threads through a small bead. Draw the outside 4 threads on left towards the small bead. DHH diagonally to the right with the 5th thread. Repeat on the right side.
Make an overhand knot with all threads. Leave about 3 inches of thread, put a small bead on each, make an overhand knot, cut near the knot and secure with a little glue.

To finish
Undo the knots on the foundation threads. On each side * thread a small bead onto the 2 center 36 inch lengths, and using these lengths as a core make 5 square knots. Repeat from * until necklace is the desired length.
For a fastening, make a buttonhole loop at one end by working half hitches over one of the foundation threads with one thread, then work half hitches on an opposite foundation thread with the 4th thread and attach a large bead at the other end. Make a final overhand knot at each end and cut close to the knot, securing with a little glue.

7 Beaded vest

You will need
600 yds thin rattail cord or 3 skeins Tempo Nova rayon cord
21 large ceramic beads
294 small ceramic beads
Strip of white felt

Measurements
To fit 36in bust
Neck to hem at back 21in
Fringe 10in

How to make the vest
The vest is made in 3 pieces, the 2 fronts and the back. Buy a suitable pattern in the right size, cut off the seam allowance, and tape both fronts to working surface. Mark both patterns identically in one inch squares.
Cut 2 strips of white felt 5 inches by ½ inch and turn it under ½ inch at each end. Embroider 18 chain stitches down the middle of the strips with a length of rattail or rayon cord. Pin these strips at the top of each shoulder. These form the seam and the lengths for the fronts are attached on the front of the chain stitches, and those for the back are attached on the back of the chain stitches.
*Cut 18 lengths each 192 inches, double and attach to row of chain stitches. Take the last 2 threads on the right and using the inside thread as a leader, DHH vertically over it with the outside thread to form a braid, (the length of the braid throughout the pattern will depend on the positioning of the next row of diagonal cording directly underneath). Using the 2nd, 15th, 16th, 29th and 30th threads from the left as leaders, DHH diagonally over the next 6 threads to the left and right respectively. Take the first 2 threads on the left and work vertical DHH using the inside thread as a leader. Counting from the right, divide the threads hanging from the diagonal DHH into groups of 12 and make a square knot using the 8 center threads as a core. This will make 2 square knots. Cross leaders in the center and continue diagonal DHHs to form a diamond.
Continue in this way following the pattern carefully. After approximately 3 complete rows it will be necessary to increase. In order to work out the lengths of the new threads to be attached, subtract 24 inches for every 3 inches from the top of the work. Cut the lengths and attach to the braid of vertical DHHs adding the number of lengths needed to keep the figure constant throughout, i.e. so that the DHH are always knotted over 6 doubled threads and the square knots are always made with 12 threads.
Continue in this way until the work measures 16 inches and 13 whole pattern rows have been completed.*
Repeat from * to * for the right front so that it corresponds with the left front. Take work off board and replace front patterns with back pattern.
Back
Cut 18 lengths each 192 inches, double and attach to row of chain stitches. Cut a foundation thread 7½ inches and sew each end to the strips of felt at each shoulder. Cut 32 lengths each 192 inches and attach to the foundation thread. Knot the pattern as for the front increasing in the same way as described above, until the back matches the front. It should measure approximately 20 inches from the neck to the bottom of the work.
Take work off board and sew sides together.
Fringe
At the lower edge of the vest there are now 21 motifs each with 14 threads, 12 center threads and one on each side previously used as leaders. Take the 2 center threads from each of these motifs and pass a small bead onto the left thread, and each alternate thread to the left. Using the right thread as a leader, DHH diagonally to the left over all adjacent threads. Again take the 2 center threads and pass a bead onto the right thread and every alternate thread to the right. Using the left hand thread as a leader DHH diagonally to the right over all adjacent threads.
Take the center 6 threads and make a square knot. Pass a large bead through the 2 center threads and make another square knot over 6 threads. Using the outside threads on each side as leaders DHH diagonally into the center. DHH the right leader over the left leader. Pass a small bead on each alternate thread and ** DHH diagonally into the center once again.** Pass a small bead onto the

2 leaders and repeat from ** to **. Make an overhand knot with 4 center threads. Trim fringe to 10 inches.

8 Necklace

You will need
50yds thin rattail or Tempo Nova rayon cord
Matching sewing thread

Measurements
15in, excluding fringe
Length of front fringe, 3½in
Length of back fringe, 2½in

How to make the necklace
Cut 20 lengths of cord, each 36 inches long. Pin 10 threads to the working surface, placing each pin 12 inches from the top end.
Counting from the left, use the 5th thread as leader and DHH diagonally to the left. Repeat with the 4th, 3rd and 2nd threads in turn. Repeat with the 6th, 7th, 8th and 9th threads as leader, this time knotting DHHs to the right.
Using 5th and 6th threads as a core and working with the 4th and 7th threads, make 3 square knots. Pass the core threads over the top of the first square knot and through to the back of the work and down behind the knots, thus forming a blackberry ball. Make one more square knot directly underneath to secure.
Repeat this pattern 12 times more, then knot the 2nd set of 10 threads in the same way.

Necklace front
Pin the 2 sides of the necklace evenly on the working surface with a ½ inch space between the last sets of DHHs.
Counting from the left, make a blackberry ball as before, using threads 9, 10, 11 and 12. Make a set of DHHs with threads 1 to 10 and another set with threads 11 to 20. Use the center threads of each set to make a square knot.
Taking the threads into 5 groups of 4, make a blackberry ball with each group. Finish off by using the left-hand thread as leader and knot 2 rows of horizontal DHHs.
N.B. If any of the threads have become too short, overlap ½ inch with one of the longer threads and stitch, then trim the threads to equal length. Trim the fringe to about 3½ inches. From the trimmed-off ends take 9 of the longest pieces, double them and attach to the last row of horizontal DHHs to thicken the fringe. Secure each knot with a tiny stitch of matching thread. Trim to level of fringe.

Necklace back
Pin the 2 sides at the other end to form a V, Use the 4 center threads of each side to make a square knot. Using threads 9 to 12, make a blackberry ball between the sets of DHHs. Make one blackberry ball below each square knot, using threads to 5 to 8 and 13 to 16. Finish with 2 rows of horizontal DHHs and fringe as before, trimming to about 2½ inches.

9 Headscarf

You will need
2 2oz. balls heavy crepe yarn

How to make the headscarf
Cut a foundation thread 168 inches, double it and pin it to the working surface. Space 2 pins 18 inches apart in the center of the thread.
Cut 96 lengths each 170 inches, double them and attach to the center 18 inches of the foundation thread.
Cut a separate leader 168 inches, double it and pin it to the working surface below the knots. Knot one row of horizontal DHHs. *Divide the threads into groups of 3 and make one square knot on each group.* Cut a 3rd length 168 inches, double it and using it as a leader knot another row of horizontal DHHs. Take the first 6 threads on the left and knot 3 rows of diagonal DHHs using the outside thread as a leader in each case. Repeat this using the 6 threads on the right. Cross leaders in the center and work 3 more rows of diagonal DHHs on the bottom left and the bottom right. Repeat this all the way along for 16 groups. Cut a length 34 inches and using it as a leader knot a row of horizontal DHH. Repeat from * to *. Cut a separate leader 84 inches and knot another row of DHH.
Leaving the 6 threads at either end (see "head-strap" below), divide the threads into groups of 4 and make 2 square knots on each group. **Leaving 2 threads at either end divide the threads into groups of 4 and make a row of single square knots alternate to the previous row. Then, including the 2 extra threads at either end make 2 square knots on each group of 4 threads alternate to the previous row. Repeat from ** to ** for approximately 6½ inches.
After working for 6½ inches it will be necessary to start decreasing the rows. Leave 2 extra threads out at the beginning and end of each previous row, so that each repeat of single and double knot rows eliminates 4 threads. Repeat this for 6 pattern repeats until there are 24 extra threads at each side. In order to make a small point take the next 20 threads from each end and make alternating rows of single and double square knots for 5 pattern repeats decreasing in the way described above at each end of each row. This will form a small point, and 20 extra threads at each side of the work. Setting these threads aside work with the remaining 92 threads. Continue working alternate rows of single and double square knots and decreasing in the way described above for 5 pattern repeats. This will leave 20 extra threads on each side.
Leaving 12 threads at each end, continue working with 28 center threads and decreasing 2 threads per row at each side to form a point.

Chin-strap
Attach extra doubled thread onto the end knot of the first row of square knots. Then, using the 2 threads from the foundation thread, the 4 threads used as leaders and the 2 threads just attached, make square knots for 15 inches. Tie an overhand knot and trim to the desired length. Tie each pair of threads in the fringe into an overhand knot 1½ inches down. Then, each separate thread should also be tied into an overhand knot a further inch down.

Head-strap
Take the 6 threads left free immediately after knotting the last row of DHHs and the ends of the 2 leaders used for the last 2 rows of DHHs. DHH the end of the first leader onto the 2nd leader. Then using the outside thread in each case as a leader, knot zig-zag diagonal DHHs across the full width for 3½ inches. Repeat on the other side of the work. Finish the strap using top 4 threads from each side as a core and the remaining threads and make a square knot. Trim ends to 3½ inches.

To finish
Cut 8 lengths each 12–14 inches. Double one thread and attach the end 2 threads of the first row of single square knots. Attach another thread onto the 6th row of single square knots. Attach the

other 2 threads onto the 7th row and the 12th row. Join the first and 2nd threads together in an overhand knot to form a pleat. Join the 3rd and 4th threads together in the same way to form another pleat. Repeat on the other side of the work. Stitch pleats together for 2 inches from the edge to secure. Make overhand knots in pairs of threads all around the scarf and trim to the desired length.

10 Persian pattern shoulder bag

You will need
One 2 oz. ball each of tan, cream, light blue, dark blue in knitting yarn
Matching darning yarn
¼yd cotton lining
Sewing thread to match lining

Measurements
8in square excluding heading and fringe
N.B. Make 2 squares of this size

How to make the bag
Cut 12 cream lengths each 90 inches, 6 lengths each of tan, light blue and dark blue, all 100 inches. Attach these threads with simple picots in the following order: *2 cream, one dark blue, one tan (cross the blue and tan picots and attach to the foundation thread alternately in the order blue, tan, blue, tan), 2 light blue, one tan, one dark blue (this time in the order tan, dark blue, tan, dark blue) 2 cream. Repeat from * 2 times more. Fix with 2 rows of horizontal DHHs, using separate foundation threads laid across.
The entire design is worked in diagonal DHHs, the rows being close together some sloping to the right and some to the left.
First row Using 2nd thread as leader, DHH to left with first thread. Using 3rd thread as leader, DHH to left over 2 threads. Using 4th thread as leader, DHH to left over 3 threads. Leave these 4 cream threads to the left. Using 6th (tan) thread as leader, DHH to left once. Using 8th (tan) thread as leader, DHH to left over 2 threads. Using 10th (light blue) thread as leader, DHH to left over 3 threads. Using 12th (light blue) thread as leader, DHH to left over 4 threads. Using 14th (dark blue) thread as leader, DHH to left over 5 threads. Using 16th (dark blue) thread as leader, DHH to left over 6 threads. Using 18th (cream) thread as leader, DHH to left over 7 threads. Using 20th (cream) thread as leader, DHH to left over 8 threads. Using 22nd (cream) thread as leader, DHH to left over 9 threads. Using 24th (cream) thread as leader, DHH to left over 10 threads.
Leave these threads and repeat this use of alternate threads as leader so that work develops in triangular points. Repeat to end of row.
2nd row DHH first 4 (cream) threads to right over 6 threads. Repeat with next group of cream threads. At the end of the row DHH the last 2 cream threads to left, then bring down next 6 colored threads to the left over themselves, starting with outside (tan) thread, and using each of the others as leader in turn. Remember that the leader always goes over the knotting thread.
3rd row DHH first 6 threads to the right, using outside thread as leader in turn. In the groups of cream threads, DHH the 4 on the right-hand side to the left. In the groups of tan and blue threads, DHH left-hand groups to the right.
4th row DHH groups of 4 cream threads to left and right as they lie.
5th row Treat first 4 cream threads as in first

39

row. DHH groups of tan and blue threads to left. DHH groups of cream threads to left. At end of row, DHH last 4 cream threads to left, using outside thread as leader in turn.

6th row Repeat as for the 4th row. Take care to continue in half patterns at the sides, as already explained. Knot the pattern for 8 inches, ending with one row of horizontal DHHs.

To finish
Trim the fringe to 3 inches.
Make a braid with 4 threads each of tan, light and dark blue, cut 90 inches. Tie a knot at each end of the braid.
With right sides together, stitch the 2 pieces of the bag up the sides, matching the pattern and using matching darning thread. Turn to the right side, part the fringe to each side and sew along the bottom of the bag.
Attach the knots of the braid level with the bottom row of horizontal DHHs on each side of the bag and stitch the braid up each side. Cut cotton lining to fit, sew up the sides and insert in the bag, turning in top and slip stitching to top row of horizontal DHHs.

11 Cavandoli watchbands

Large watch
You will need
One skein each of fuchsia and beige in Lily's Double Quick Crochet Cotton or rig warp
One buckle

Chart for man's watchband

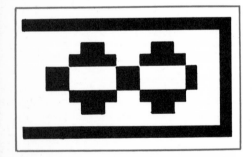

Measurements
Width, ¾in
Length to buckle, 3in
Length to tapered end, 4in

How to make the watchband
The instructions for how to work Cavandoli are shown in the Crash Course at the back of the book on page 111. Work from the charts given for each strap.
Length to buckle
Cut 5 lengths each 48 inches in fuchsia, double and attach to bar of watch. Secure watch to working surface. Cut one length of beige 144 inches and attach to left side of work. Use this thread as leader throughout. Continue knotting horizontal and vertical DHHs following the pattern from the chart. Knot picots at either side with sungold.
When the work measures 3 inches attach each of the threads to the buckle and sew in the loose ends on the wrong side. Trim closely.
Knot the other end in the same way until 3½ inches have been completed. It will now be necessary to taper the ends. Make the first vertical knot on every row over 2 threads instead of one. Pin the outside

thread to one side until the article is finished. Turn under all the loose threads and sew in at the back.

Chart for child's watchband

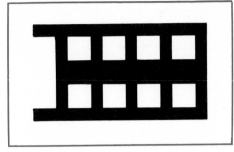

Lady's watch
You will need
One ball J & P Coat's "Knit Cro-Sheen" in tan
6 yds gold lurex
One buckle

Measurements
Width, ¾in
Length to buckle, 2½in
Length to tapered end, 4in

How to make the watchband
Length to buckle
Cut 4 lengths each 36 inches in tan, double and attach bar of watch. Secure watch to working surface. Cut one length gold 144 inches and attach to left side of work. Use this thread as a leader throughout. Continue knotting horizontal and vertical DHHs following the pattern from the chart. Make picots at either side with gold. Attach threads to buckle as for the large watchband. Knot the other end in the same way and taper at the end as for the large watchband.

Chart for lady's watchband

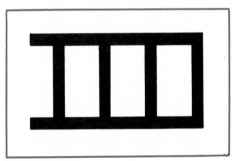

Child's watch
You will need
One ball each of tan and light blue in J & P Coat's "Knit Cro-Sheen"
One buckle

Measurements
Width, ⅜in
Length to buckle, 3in
Length to tapered end, 3½in

How to make the watchband
Length to buckle
Cut 4 lengths each 36ins in light blue, double and attach to bar of watch. Secure watch to working surface. Cut one length tan 120 inches and attach to left side of work. Use this thread as a leader throughout. Continue knotting horizontal and vertical DHHs following the pattern from the chart. Make picots at either side with tan. Attach threads to buckle as for the large watchband. Knot the other end in the same way and taper at the end as for the large watchband.

12 Hat

You will need
96 yds each of blue, green synthetic raffia (raffene)
8yds single core bell wire

Measurements
To fit average adult head, about 22½in

How to make the hat
The hat can be made over a felt hood stuffed to make a firm shape or over a wig stand or hat block – preferably something into which pins will stick. Cut the blue raffene into 34 lengths each 96 inches and the green into 34 lengths each 72 inches. The bell wire is used as leader for horizontal DHH throughout, spiraling from center crown to brim edge.
Crown
Make a tiny loop in the end of the bell wire and pin to center of working surface. Attach 8 doubled blue lengths, curl the wire around a finger and pin the circle formed to working surface. Spiral the wire around this first circle ½ inch out.
DHH the blue threads over the wire leader on each circle, adding extra lengths as required to keep wire completely covered. Continue in this way until there are 6 spirals in all.
From the 7th spiral increase the distance to one inch and attach green threads between each pair of blue threads.
Continue DHHs knotting 2 threads blue alternated with 2 threads green for 5 circles more.
Band
The point where the first green threads were introduced is the back of the hat. Even with this point, between the last DHH spiral made and the next spiral, make the first half only of a square knot 7 times to make a spiral braid, using 2 green threads as core and 2 blue threads as knotting threads.
Brim
Position the next 3 spirals at a distance of 2 inches each. Fill the area with alternated square knots, and alternating the colors i.e. first row blue threads as core, green threads as knotting threads; next row green threads as core and blue threads as knotting threads.
DHH over each spiral as it is reached, making extra knots with each thread if required, to cover the wire completely. On the last spiral, DHH each thread 3 times instead of twice.

To finish
Make an overhand knot on pairs of the same color, all around. Trim ends.

13 Sash and headband

You will need
140 yds Lily fine nylon macramé cord
One gold ring, 1¾in diameter
8 very large glass beads
6 medium glass beads
12 small glass beads (headband)

Measurements
Sash. To fit 38in hip, adjustable
Width, 3½in
Fringe, 24in
Headband. 22in excluding fringe
Width, 1½in
Fringe, 12in

How to make the sash

Cut 10 lengths each 192 inches. Attach them onto the ring with the knots to the back of the work (see diagram)

Attaching lengths onto ring

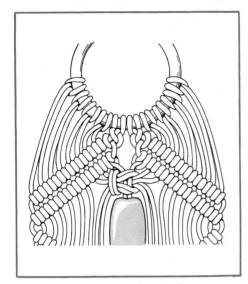

*Using 2 center lengths leaders, DHH diagonally out to left and right. Knot a 2nd row of DHHs directly under each one just worked. Using the 2 center threads as a core, make a square knot with the 2 threads on either side of the core. Pass the 2 core threads through a large bead. Secure with one square knot under the bead.

Using the outside thread at each side as leader, DHH diagonally into the center. Knot a 2nd row of DHHs directly under each one just knotted.* Repeat from * to * 3 more times, crossing the leaders in the center of the last 2 rows of diagonal DHHs.** DHH out horizontally to left and right Thread a small bead onto the 2 center threads. Using the outside thread at each side as leader, DHH diagonally into the center directly under the bead. Cross the leaders.** Repeat from ** to ** twice more.

Tie all threads in an overhand knot 2½ inches below the last row of DHHs. Trim the ends to 24 inches from the knot and unravel to form a fringe.

N.B. The belt can be adjusted to fit any hip size by omitting or adding pattern repeats.

Turn the work and make a 2nd side to correspond with the first.

How to make the headband

Cut 6 lengths each 96 inches and 2 lengths each 144 inches. Cut one length 60 inches of yarn or embroidery floss in a matching color on which to thread the beads in case the hole is very fine or irregular.

Lay out all the threads so that the ends are even at the top and make an overhand knot 12 inches down. Pin each thread to the work surface, placing the bead thread in the center and the 96 inch threads at each outer edge and the 144 inch threads next to them.

Begin work 4 inches below the overhand knot and using the bead thread as a core, make a square knot with one thread from either side.

Using these 2 threads as leaders, DHH diagonally out to right and left.

Using bead thread as a core, make a square knot with one thread from either side. Thread a bead onto the center thread and secure with one square knot. Using the outside threads as leaders, DHH diagonally back into the center, cross the right leader over the left one in the middle and DHH diagonally out to the sides again. Repeat from * to * 11 times but omit the last diagonal DHH rows out to the sides on the last repeat. Make an

overhand knot 4 inches from the work and trim ends to correspond with the other end.

14 Choker

You will need
55yds rayon cord or thin rattail
1 square inch Velcro
Knotting board
Pins, scissors, needle and matching thread

How to make the choker
Cut 6 strands of yarn, each 104 inches long. Cut another length about 6 inches, double it and pin it to the board to form a foundation thread. Double the lengths of cord and knot them onto the foundation thread.

Knot 2 rows of horizontal DHHs as follows: using the first knotting thread as a leader, knot a row of DHH knots across from left to right. Secure the leader thread at the right-hand side with a pin, turn the thread, and knot another row of DHH knots from right to left. (Do not use a separate foundation thread for these rows of horizontal DHHs as the cord is usually bulky to sew in at the back.)

Using the outside thread on the right as a leader, DHH diagonally into the center. Using the outside thread on the left as a leader knot diagonal DHHs from left to right across all 11 knotting threads. Take up the right-hand leader again, and complete the first diagonal bar from the center to the left.

Repeat this procedure until the length of the choker is the same as your neck measurement, then work as follows: on the next row of diagonal DHHs into the center, work from right to left over five knotting threads, and then from left to right over 6 threads. Now bring the outside threads down as leaders from the right and left, and knot 4 rows of diagonal DHH into the center alternately from right and left to make a pointed end.

To finish
Turn back the threads and sew them down at the back of the work for about a ¼ inch, then trim the ends closely. Do the same with the foundation threads. Separate the piece of Velcro, and sew one half to each end of the choker, trimming the Velcro to fit.

15 Beaded cotton jacket

You will need
1000 yds Coats and Clark's O.N.T. Pearl Cotton 3 or 10/5 linen
About 600 medium beads
A blouse pattern one size smaller than is usually worn
Crochet hook

How to make the jacket
The jacket is made in 5 pieces which are crocheted or overcast together. If you find difficulty in obtaining beads of the desired color, use plain wooden ones (colored if plain are unobtainable), string them up and spray with spray enamel paint, being careful to protect the surface behind the beads with a sheet of paper.

Preparing the pattern
Cut off the seam allowances on the blouse pieces. Make a 2nd sleeve, reversing the shape. If the blouse front is in one piece, cut it in half to give a left and right front. If already in 2 pieces, trim to the center front line and make a 2nd, reversed front.

Take the 5 pieces (right front, left front, back and 2 sleeves) and mark them off in one inch squares on the right side. Start at the center front line of the fronts, the center back of the back and the center of the sleeves.

Draw a colored line across at armhole level of all 5 of the pattern pieces.

Setting up the board
The board should be slightly larger than the biggest pattern piece.

Start with the right front and tape this onto the board, making the center front line parallel with the edge of the board.

Crochet a length of chain to go around the sides and top of the pattern piece plus 6 inches.

Pin the chain around the pattern, starting at the bottom left hand corner and leaving 3 inches hanging below the lower edge, thus allowing a safety margin. Pin up the left side, around the armhole, shoulder seam, neck edge and down the center front, again leaving 3 inches surplus.

Attach doubled threads at the shoulder line, knotting them into the crochet chain. The threads when doubled should be 4 times the finished length of the jacket, including fringe. Knot one doubled thread into the first chain, skip a chain, knot into each of the next 2 chain, *skip one chain, knot into each of the next 2 chain, repeat from * along neck edge where another single thread is positioned. Begin working in groups of alternating double square knots keeping the knots even with the horizontal lines on the pattern paper and pinning each knot in place as it is made. The threads are slipped through the crochet chain at the sides as the work progresses.

Attach new doubled threads as required in the crochet chain around the neck and armhole edges. Continue in this way down to the colored line at armhole level.

Making the pattern
On all the pieces, the pattern begins at the bottom of the armhole shaping where the colored line is drawn. The pattern is positioned outward from the center front on the fronts, the center back on the back and from the center line of each sleeve, It is easier to see the pattern if the beads are first pinned in position over the pattern piece on the board and threaded in as the work progresses. The pattern begins at the top with points, one bead at the apex, then 2 beads and then a row of beads alternated with square knots, and then a complete row of beads only. The beads are threaded horizontally, except on the row which is beads only, and these are threaded alternately vertically and horizontally. Under this there are 2 rows of double beading and then the pattern is knotted to form an uneven edge before the fringe.

Completing the fronts
When the right front is completed, leave the threads hanging and take the whole piece and the pattern paper off the board. Tape the left front pattern onto the board and work as before, making sure both sides match.

Making the back
The back is worked on the same principle as the fronts, taping the pattern onto the board and pinning a crochet chain around the side and top edges with a 3 inch surplus at each end.

Attach the doubled threads at the shoulder seams and work around the neck shaping, adding new threads as required. Where the knotting meets at the center back it may be necessary to make slight adjustments to the distance between the knots. Begin patterning at armhole the same level as before.

The threads slipped through the crochet chain

Attaching new threads to form the shaping

Making the sleeves
Knot the sleeves from the top, increasing as before and placing the pattern in the center.

To finish
Crochet or overcast the pieces together. Work double crochet all around the neck and front edges to strengthen, at the same time working chain loops down the right front edge for buttonholes. Stitch beads to correspond down the left front for buttons.
Finally trim the fringe and secure, fasten off crochet chain.

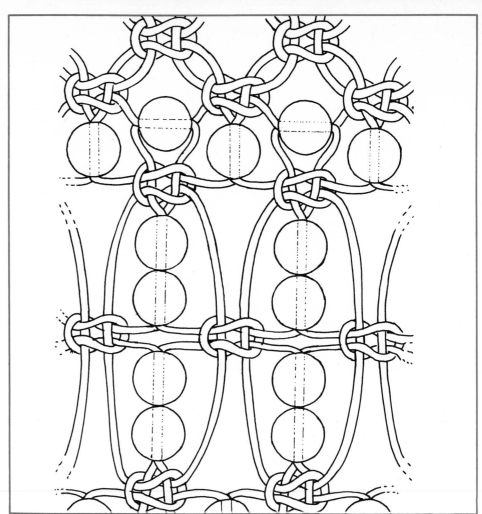

The completely beaded row is threaded horizontally and vertically

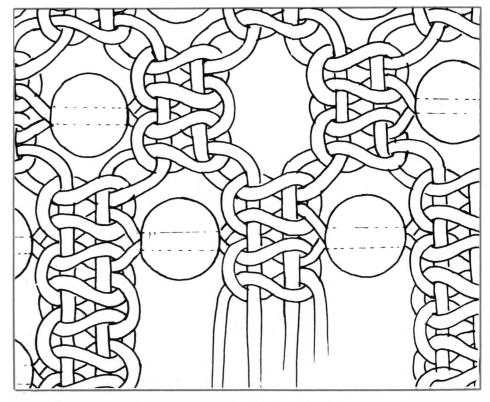

The formation of the uneven edge worked before the fringing

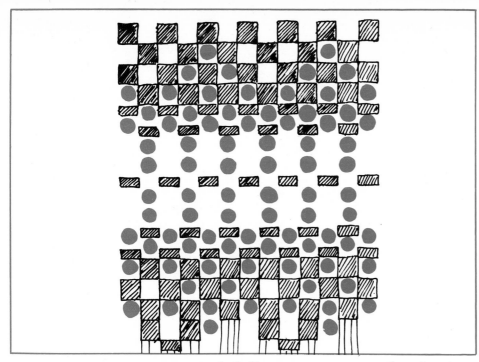

Complete bead pattern, each full square representing two square knots

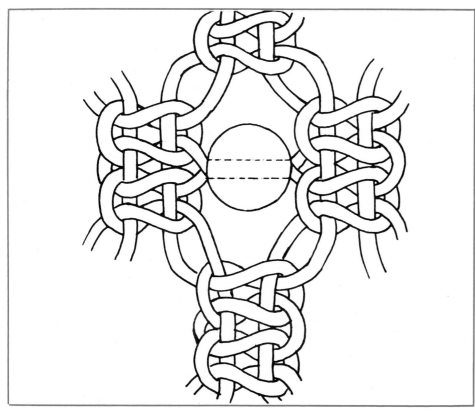

The method of threading the beads horizontally into the work

You will need
50yds each of pink, purple, green in
thin rattail or Tempo Nova rayon cord
Buckle
Small piece Velcro

Measurements
Belt. 26 in by 1¾in
Bracelet. 8in by 1¾in
Each repeat measures 1½in

How to make the belt
Cut 2 pink lengths each 24 inches, 2 purple lengths
each 24 inches and 4 green lengths each 15 inches.
Attach threads onto loop end of buckle as follows:
2 green, one pink, 2 purple, one pink and
2 green.
Using 2nd thread from left as leader, DHH
diagonally to the left over next thread. Using 15th
thread from left, DHH diagonally to the right
over next thread.
Using 4th thread from left as leader, DHH
diagonally to the left over next 3 threads. Using
13th thread from left, DHH diagonally to the
right over next 3 threads.
Using each green thread in turn as leader, DHH
diagonally to the center over next 8 threads,
beginning with the inner green thread of each set.
*Using 4 center green threads as core, make a
square knot with the 2 green threads on either side.
Using each green thread in turn as leader, DHH
diagonally out to the sides over next 8 threads,
beginning with the outer green thread of each set.
Using 4 center purple threads as core, make a
square knot with the 2 pink threads on either side.
Using each green thread in turn as leader, DHH
diagonally into center as before.*
Repeat from * to * 14 times more.
N.B. Adjust length here, allowing 24 inches of extra
cord for each additional pattern repeat.
Using top right-hand green leaders to continue as
leader DHH to left over next 4 threads. Using
inner left-hand green thread as leader DHH
diagonally to right over next 3 threads. Using next
green thread from right-hand set as leader, DHH
diagonally to left over next 3 threads. Using next
green thread from left-hand set as leader, DHH
diagonally to right over next 2 threads. Using next
green thread from right-hand set as leader, DHH
diagonally to left over next 2 threads. Using next
green thread from left-hand set as leader, DHH
diagonally to right over next thread. Using next
green thread from right-hand set as leader, DHH
diagonally to left over next thread.
Using 2nd pink thread from left as leader, DHH
diagonally to right over next thread. Using outer
pink thread at right-hand edge as leader, DHH
diagonally to left over next thread. Using outer
pink thread at left-hand edge as leader, DHH
diagonally over next 2 threads. Sew in ends.
How to make the bracelet
Cut 2 pink lengths each 9 inches, 2 purple lengths
each 9 inches and 4 green lengths each 8 inches.
Attach to green foundation thread as for belt.
Make as for belt repeating from * to * 3 times
more instead of 14.
Complete as for belt.

To finish
Belt. Slot pointed end through buckle bar and
stitch in place.
Bracelet. Sew in ends of foundation thread.
Stitch a small piece of Velcro under pointed end
and on right side of square end.

17 Fringed shawl

You will need
300 yds thin rattail or Tempo Nova rayon cord
1yd 36in wide fabric
1yd 36in wide lining fabric
Brown paper 17in by 30in
350 small wooden beads
31 large wooden beads

Measurements
Center back 20in, excluding fringe
Center back neck to lower front edge
17½in, excluding fringe
Fringe 7½in

How to make the shawl
Cut a rectangle of brown paper 17 inches by 30 inches and lay it on a flat surface with the 17 inch edges at the top and bottom. Mark the left

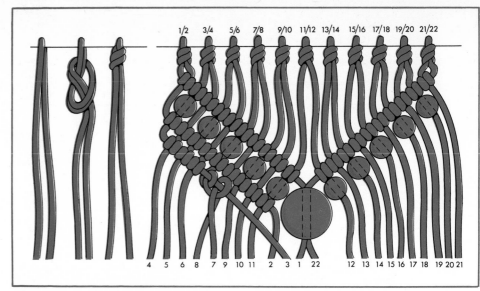

Drawing out the pattern

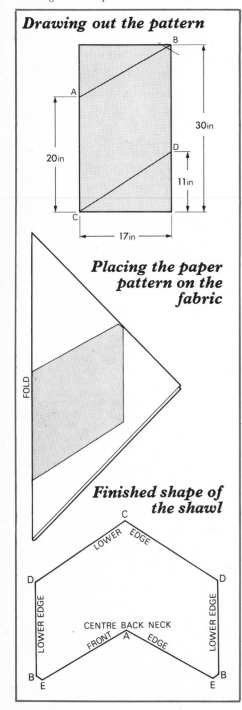

Placing the paper pattern on the fabric

Finished shape of the shawl

Attaching threads with overhand knots

edge 20½ inches up from the bottom corner and the right edge 11 inches up from the bottom corner. Draw a pencil line from the left edge marking to the top right-hand corner (A–B), and from the right edge marking to the bottom left corner (C–D), thus forming a slanting diamond shape. Mark A–D as fold line, then cut along A–B and C–D. Measure and mark one inch down each line from point B, join the 2 points and cut along the line. Fold fabric into a triangle and lay the fold line of the paper pattern to the fold line of the fabric. Pin the pattern in place. Cut one piece of main fabric and one lining.
Place fabric and lining wrong sides together and stitch all around, taking a ¼ inch seam allowance, and leaving a 6 inch gap on the A–B edge. Turn right sides out through this gap, then slip stitch open edges together. Baste all around edges through both thicknesses and press.

Macrame edging
Cut 345 strands each 30 inches. This can be done quickly by winding the cord around a piece of stiff cardboard 30 inches long. Tie the threads on each side of the cardboard with separate lengths of cord and cut the cords at each end of the cardboard. Each scallop has 11 doubled threads attached to a width of 2¼ inches with ⅛ inch space between the scallops. Thread each length into a large needle and insert it through the fabric about ⅛ inch from the edge. Remove the needle and adjust the ends of the cord so that they are even before tying an overhand knot close to the fabric edge.
Begin at center point C. Attach one thread on the exact point, then 6 threads evenly on each side of the center thread to form the first scallop.

Scallop
Using outside threads as leaders, DHH diagonally into the center over 10 threads. Pass both leaders through the center of a large bead.
Counting from the outer edges in, put a small bead on every 2nd thread. Using outside threads as leaders, DHH diagonally over 9 threads.
Using outside threads as leaders, knot a 2nd row of DHHs over 9 threads. Make an overhand knot with the 4 center threads directly under the large bead.

Positioning the scallops
Make 7 scallops on each side of the center one. At the D corners, attach one thread at the point of the corner with 6 threads on each side of it, thus making the scallop over 13 threads with 6 small beads on each side, to weight these corners. Continue from D to B on both sides of the shawl, making 6 more complete scallops and ending with

Working the horizontal DHH of the scallop

the 7th and final scallop set with 6 threads on the remaining part of the straight edge D–B, and 5 threads attached to the one inch cut-off corners (marked on the diagram as B–E).

To finish
Measure 5 inches from the bottom of the overhand knot under each big bead and trim all along fringe. Remove basting threads.

18 Leather bracelet

You will need
16ft of ⅜in wide leather thonging
One strip leather 9in by 1½in

Measurements
9in by 1¾in

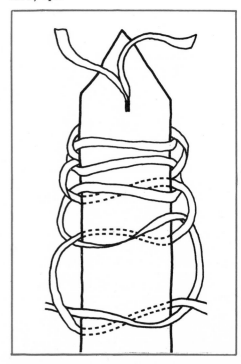

Make square knots over a strip of leather

How to make the bracelet

Place the ends of the leather strip together and trim the double thickness to a point from ¾ inch down.

Pierce a hole with the pointed blade of a pair of scissors ¼ inch below each point. By using this method rather than a leather punch, the hole will grip the ends of the leather thonging firmly.

Cut the thonging into 2 lengths each 96 inches. Push both ends through one of the pierced holes from back to front leaving about 5 inches on the right side. Knot the thonging into square knots, using the leather strip as the core. Be careful to keep the leather flat. This can be done by pinning the top end to a board through the pierced hole and passing a length of string through the other hole and tying it to the waist.

Continue the square knots until the level of the 2nd pierced knot. Pass the thongs through from back to front and trim to leave about 5 inches.

19 Little girl's jumper

You will need
3 2oz. balls double crepe yarn
1 2oz ball (as above) in contrasting color
3 buttons

Measurements
To fit 6–8 year olds
Waistband 24in

How to make the jumper
Waistband
Cut a foundation thread 20 inches in the main color, double it and pin to working surface. Cut 7 lengths 200 inches in main color and one length 200 inches in contrasting color, Attach the 8 lengths onto the foundation thread starting with the contrasting color on the left. Cut another length 300 inches of main color, doubled and attach to the right hand side of the work. * Using this thread as a leader knot 4 rows of horizontal DHHs. Take the first 10 threads on the left and make a square knot using 6 center threads as a core. Make a square knot on the remaining 8 threads using the 4 center threads as a core.* Repeat from * to * 16 more times, so that there are 17 patterns. Leaving out 4 threads at each side of the work, make a square knot with the rest of the threads. Knot 2 more rows of DHHs on each side of the square knot starting with the 4 free threads on either side. Turn back ends of DHHs and darn into the work.

Skirt
Cut 166 lengths each 144 inches in main color and attach to the waistband. Divide threads into groups of 4 and work 3 rows of alternating square knots. On alternate rows at each end work one vertical DHH knot in order to keep the sides firm. Working from the right on the 4th row make 9 square knots. Leave out the rest of the threads and go back to the right. Continue making alternating square knots within this section eliminating 2 threads at the beginning and the end of each row, until you have only one knot. Continue in this way all around the skirt until 9 points are formed, but use 8 knots for each pattern except the last one on the left, which will again have 9. (This extra width allows for an overlap at the back fastening.)
Using the top threads on each side of the 9 groups as leaders DHH diagonally down the edge to the point. Divide the threads into groups of 4 and make a square knot on each group. Knot another

row of diagonal DHHs to the point.
Starting at the top points make rows of alternating square knots down to one row below the bottom points. Remove work from board and place it around a pillow or 24 inch board so that it can be worked as a circular pattern.
Make rows of alternating square knots overlapping ¼ inch at the back for the placket. Make the square knots farther apart as the work continues down in order to shape the skirt. The knots should be ½ inch apart and continue getting farther apart until they are ¾ inch apart. Work in this way for 4 inches and the make a 2 inch border of square knots that are more closely spaced. Divide the threads into groups of 2 and make an overhand knot with each pair. Cut fringe to the desired length.

Straps
Cut 4 lengths 208 inches in main color and 2 lengths 208 inches in contrasting color. Measuring from front center of skirt skip 2 holes in the waistband and attach lengths for strap as follows: 2 main color, 2 contrasting color, 2 main color. Make alternating square knots for 19 inches. On the next row skip the center knot to make the buttonhole.** Continue alternating square knots for one inch** and make a second buttonhole. Repeat from ** to ** and make a 3rd buttonhole. Make one row of square knots. Divide the threads into groups of 4 and make an overhand knot on each group. Trim to the desired length. Make

2nd strap to match the first.
Make another 2 straps in the same way 4¼ inches long in alternating square knots without the buttonholes. Sew one strap to each long strap 2 inches above waistband. Sew 2nd short strap to long straps 1¼ inches above the first. Make 2 tassels 3 inches long and attach to the bottom of each long strap at the waistband. Sew 3 buttons on the back to correspond with buttonholes. (N.B. If waistband is a little wide, make a square knot braid in contrasting color and thread it through the slots in the waistband and tie it at the back or front.)

20 Pants suit panels and cuffs

N.B. The macramé panels and cuffs can be added to any pants suit.

You will need
200 yds thin rattail or 10/5 linen or acrylic knitting yarn

Measurements
Side panels. 14in by 2¼in, adjustable
Cuffs. 7in by 2in, adjustable

How to make the side panels
Cut 10 lengths each 112 inches and one foundation thread 12 inches. Attach doubled lengths to foundation thread.
Make rows of alternated square knots for 14 inches.
Knot 2 rows of horizontal DHHs, using left and right hand threads alternately as leaders.
Divide threads into 5 groups of 4 threads each and make one overhand knot on each group. Using 2 left-hand groups together, make one overhand knot with 8 threads. Using the 2 right-hand groups together, make one overhand knot with 8 threads. Trim fringe to about 5 inches.

How to make the cuffs
Cut 10 lengths each 66 inches.
Take 4 threads together and make 6 square knots in the center of these threads. Pin square knots to working surface to form a loop. Take inner thread from each end of loop and pin across under loop (see diagram a). Using these threads as leaders, knot horizontal DHHs with remaining threads. Attach remaining 6 lengths in center of the leaders (see diagram b).
Make 33 rows of alternating square knots.
Using the right-hand thread as leader, knot one row of horizontal DHHs across all threads.
Divide threads into 2 groups of 10 threads each.

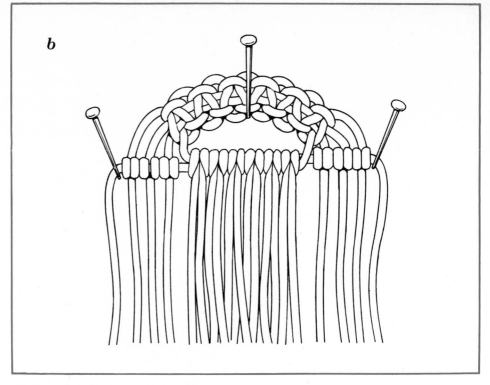

On the left-hand group, using the outer 3 threads together as leader, knot one row of diagonal DHHs into the center, using the thread in pairs, across the next 3 pairs. Using outer 2 threads together as leader, knot one row of diagonal DHHs into the center, across next 2 pairs. Make right-hand side to correspond.
Take all 20 threads together to tie an overhand knot. Pull each thread separately to tighten knot. Trim fringe to about 3 inches.

21 Necklace

You will need
(same as for panels and cuffs)
34 beads

Measurements
19in, excluding fringe
Front panel. 5in wide

How to make the necklace
Cut 12 lengths each 147 inches and 6 lengths each 48 inches.
Pass 2 of the long lengths through 2 beads and position the beads at the center of the threads. Then pass all 4 ends through a 3rd bead (see diagram c). Divide these 4 threads into 2 groups of 2 and set 2 more long lengths on each group (see diagram c).
Make 47 rows alternated square knots.
Using 4 more of the long lengths, make a square knot loop as given for cuff.
Knot horizontal DHHs and attach remaining 2 lengths as given for cuff.
Make 45 rows alternated square knots.
Pin these 2 pieces to working surface so that they are parallel, and one inch apart.
Using left-hand thread as leader, knot one row of horizontal DHHs across left-hand thread, take leader across one inch space and then continue horizontal DHHs across right-hand threads.
Attach 48 inch lengths on leader at one inch intervals. Divide threads into 9 groups of 4 threads each. Make 3 square knots on each group. Place a bead on the core threads of each group and secure with one square knot. Using right-hand thread as leader, knot one row of horizontal DHHs across all threads.
Using outer thread at each side as leader, knot the next thread over it vertically 7 times.
On the next 6 threads at each side knot a diagonal DHH cross. On the next 2 threads in at each side, knot as for the outer 2 threads.
Divide remaining threads into 4 groups of 4 and make one square knot on each group. Place a bead

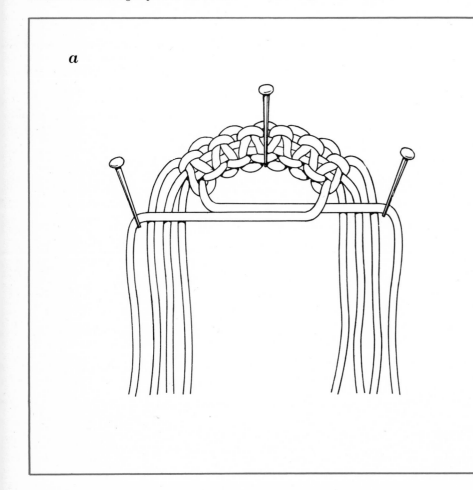

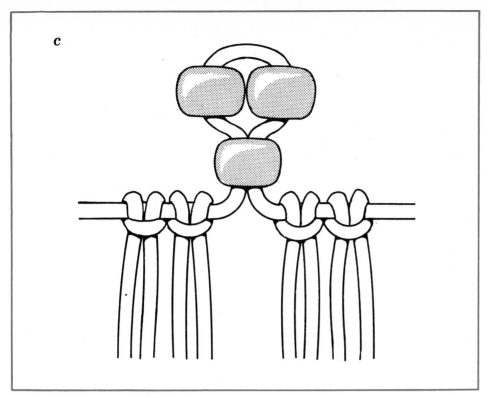

c

Detail of the necklace. Notice the back fastening

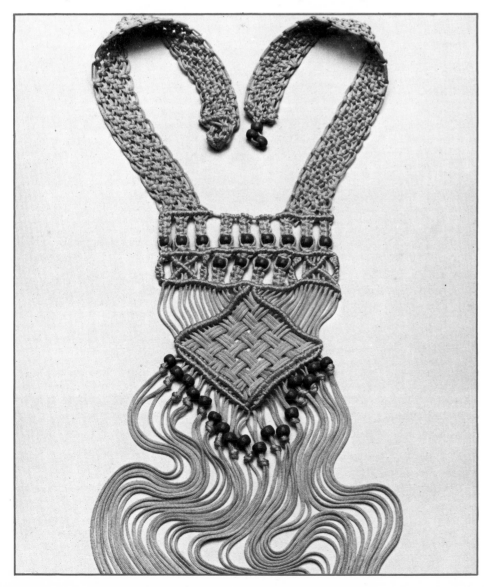

on the core threads of each group and secure with 3 square knots.

Using left-hand thread as leader, knot one row of horizontal DHHs across all threads. Using the center left-hand thread as leader, DHH diagonally to the left across all threads. Using the center right-hand thread as leader, DHH diagonally to the right across all threads.

Take the inner 3 threads of the left-hand side and weave them over the inner 3 threads of the right-hand group, under the next 3, over the next 3, under the next 3, over the next 3 and under the last 2. Continue weaving each group of 3 threads in the same way to form a diamond, ending by weaving 2 of the last 3 threads. Use the outer thread at each side as leader to DHH diagonally into the center. Using the outer threads at each side as leaders, DHH a 2nd diagonal row into the center on each side.

Divide threads into groups of 2 and put a bead on each group. Secure with an overhand knot on each group one inch away from the last row of DHHs. Trim fringe to about 9 inches.

22 *Evening bag*

You will need
2 skeins Lily Double Quick Crochet Cotton
8in nylon dress zipper
¼yd cotton for lining
Sewing thread to match

Measurements
8in by 5in

How to make the bag
The bag measures 8 inches by 5 inches, so cut out a piece of fabric 8 inches wide and 10 inches long.
Attach 48 double threads making sure the threads are 40 inches and the leaders 100 inches.
Start with 4 rows of horizontal DHHs, then knot 9 inches diagonal DHHs and finish off with 4 rows of horizontal DHHs. Darn the threads into the back of the work and trim them off. When the half-way mark is reached, stop and make sure that the fabric is straight.
Stitch up the sides matching the diamonds.
Stitch in the zipper with 2 rows of stitches, one row between the top 2 DHH rows and one over the top row.
Make the tassel through the hole in the zipper tab.

23 *Silver lurex belt and bracelet*

N.B. The finished belt is worn inside-out.

You will need
110yds silver lurex
3 pearl buttons (bracelet)

Measurements
Belt. Length 25in, excluding tassels
Belt. Length 25in. excluding tassels
Width, 1¾in
Tassels, 14½in
Bracelet. Circumference, 8in
Length of tassel, 4in

How to make the belt

Cut one length 190 inches, 2 lengths 136 inches and 13 lengths 182 inches. Pin the threads at center point to the working surface to make one half of belt first, in the following order: left to right, one 182 inch length, one 136 inch length, 12 182 inch lengths, one 136 inch length and then the 190 inch length. Divide the threads into groups of 4 and make 2 square knots on each group. Make alternated square knots for 14 rows.

Make another row of alternated square knots but eliminate the center knot, thus making only 2 knots.

Using the group of 4 threads on either side, make 8 square knots on each group. Using the center 4 threads as a core, knot the 2 threads on either side into a square knot even with the center of the 8 square knots.

Knot from *to* again below the 8 square knots.**
Knot 3 rows alternating square knots.
Knot from * to * once more.
Knot from ** to ** once more, then from * to *.
Knot 3 rows alternated square knots.
Using outer right-hand thread as leader throughout, knot 10 rows horizontal DHHs. Divide the threads into groups of 4 and make a spiral knotted chain for 13 inches and ending with an overhand knot on each group.
Trim ends to 1½ inches.
Unpin and turn work. Complete 2nd half to correspond with the first half, beginning with 2 square knots.

How to make the bracelet

Cut 4 lengths each 30 inches and 2 lengths each 100 inches.
Double the 30 inch lengths and pin to working surface to use as a core.
Position the 100 inch lengths in the center behind these and use to make 16 square knots beginning ½ inch down from the top of the loop of the core (see diagram).
Thread a pearl button onto one of the center cords. Make 3 square knots to secure.
Repeat from * to * twice.
Make 13 square knots.
Unpin the work and thread the center cords through the loop made at the beginning.
Make 3 square knots to secure.
Tie all 12 threads together in an overhand knot.
Trim tassel to measure 3 inches from knot.

Make square knots half an inch down from the top of the loop

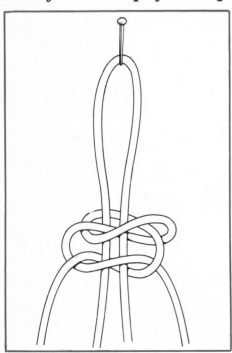

You will need
200yds thin rattail cord or Tempo Nova rayon cord
One 6in zipper
Lining fabric 7in by 7in
Matching sewing thread
One purchased belt up to 2in wide

Measurements
Width, 7in
Length excluding fringe, 7in
Fringe, 9in

How to make the bag
Front
Cut 23 lengths each 108 inches and one length 192 inches. Fold the 192 inch length so that one end is 54 inches and the other end is 138 inches. Attach these lengths doubled onto a foundation thread, placing the long piece on the right-hand edge. Throughout the work this thread will act as leader for the horizontal DHHs.
*Knot 2 rows of horizontal DHHs. Divide the threads into groups of 4 and make 2 square knots on each group. Make another 2 rows of horizontal DHHs.
Divide the threads into groups of 12 and knot a double diagonal cross. Repeat from * once more.
Knot 2 rows of horizontal DHH. Divide the threads into groups of 4. Make 2 square knots on each group. Make another 2 rows of horizontal cording.
Divide the threads into groups of 4. Starting from the left, make 2 square knots on each of the first 2 groups, 3 square knots on each of the next 2 groups, 4 square knots on the next group and 5 on the next. Reverse the sequence by working 4 square knots on the next group and so on, to end of the row. Knot 2 rows of horizontal DHHs.
Leave 9 inches for the fringing and trim.
Belt loops
Cut 7 lengths 120 inches and one length 204 inches. Divide into groups of 4 (the group with the long thread should be even at one end, the longer piece hanging from the other end) and make 4 inches of square knots in the middle.
Fold each knotted braid in half and attach to the foundation thread for the back with DHH knots, positioning one braid at each end with the long thread on the right.
Back
Cut 16 lengths 108 inches, double and set onto the foundation thread between the belt loops.
Complete the back as given for the front, using the long cord from the belt loops for the leader.

To finish
Position fabric so that the zipper lies along the top. stitch around the edges of the lining leaving a ½ inch seam allowance and incorporating into it the ends of the zipper.
Fasten off all the ends of the macramé to the back of the work.
With zipper open, slip stitch lining to back of the attached knots of the macramé, one side to the front piece, the other to the back piece.
With matching sewing thread, overcast the sides of the macramé bag on the right side. At the lower edge of the bag catch stitch between the last 2 rows of horizontal DHHs, catching in the lining.
Fringing can be added to the lower bar of the belt buckle to give a matching look. Here, attached knots have been used and secured with one overhand knot.

25

The ideal gift for Christmas or birthday. these gay paperweights in many colors can be adapted to any pattern and color. Make them as you will!

26

This beautiful hanging
lampshade made in
white cotton, is made
of three different panels,
It would look equally
effective hung over a table
or used on a standard
lamp.

A pretty glasses case to make in a few hours. Make it for yourself, or as a gift for someone special.

A covered bottle for summer picnics and parties. The beaded cover is made in polypropylene twine which is both economical and easy to work with. Try adapting the pattern to fit your favorite bottle shape.

29

Make use of any extra shells, beads or cork bottle tops that you may have stored away and hang them inside this macramé mobile.

30

A pillow in Teheran pattern worked almost entirely in diagonal DHHs. It would fit in with any furniture, modern or traditional.

31

This attractive set of placemats and napkin rings are made with nylon twine to make them hard wearing and heat proof. The two-tone effect will go with a table cloth in any color.

32

If you know any guitarists, then this is the ideal gift and is bound to be a success. If not, then why not adapt the pattern for a belt or wall hanging.

33

Add a touch of sophistication to your home with this beautiful lampshade. The subtle coloring would blend in with any furniture.

Choose your favorite
pattern and make one of
these Cavandoli rugs as
a doormat or to decorate a
small alcove.

36

A simple lampshade
worked in string and
attached to a frame.
Notice how the pattern
formation of the knots
shows up so well against
a lining.

37

This chunky wall hanging
in rug yarn is hung from
a brass rod with pointed
finials. Easy to make, it
would be the piece de
résistence of any home.

38

A cuddly pillow in felt and yarn. Quick to make, it would look beautiful in your bedroom.

39

Add color and comfort to a little stool with this macramé pad. It will make work in the garden much more pleasant.

40

Relax in your rocking chair with this padded headrest and seat. If your chair is brown, then why not work the macramé in beiges and tans.

Any dog would be more than delighted with this leash and collar! They are quick and cheap to make and made in natural twine look good against any coat.

A simple macramé braid can make an attractive and unusual holder for hanging containers. These look pretty with trailing plants and candles, bringing a touch of originality to a balcony or a patio.

43

This beautiful curtain hanging can be put up over doors or used simply as a wall decoration. Make it in your own design or use the instructions as a guide.

44

*A simple pillow made
in natural colored yarn
can add a touch of
elegance to any room.*

45

*Knotted in horizontal and
diagonal DHHs, you can
make this fringe as long
or as short as you like to
match your own window.*

46

An impressive decoration for any fireplace, this screen can be made with natural twine or dyed to the color you desire. A lining in a contrasting color looks most effective.

48

A practical item for the home can look great if you cover it in macramé. Choose a waste paper basket in any color and match it to your knotting.

47

This lampshade is decorated with rings, an idea which can be adapted for other patterns.

49

A set of placemats and napkin rings made in the round. Use them for outdoor meals in the summer.

Instructions for designs 25~50

25 Paper-weights

Paper-weight I, Kingfisher
You will need
*One skein Lily's Double Quick Crochet Cotton
One 3in bull's-eye glass paperweight
*Colored paper
*Plastic curtain ring ¾in diameter
*Felt or Suede
*Glue
*Required for all paper-weights

How to make the paper-weight
Glue colored paper to base of paper-weight in design of your choice. Cut 18 lengths each 24 inches, double each length and attach to plastic ring.
Divide threads into groups of 4 and make 5 square knots on each group.
Taking 2 threads of each group together with 2 threads of the next group to alternate the grouping, make 3 square knots on each newly formed group, positioning the first knot ¾ inch below original groups (see diagram a).

Leave ¼ inch space before continuing for 5 square knots more. Make a blackberry ball with these 5 square knots, taking core into ¼-inch space. Secure with 3 square knots. Cut 9 lengths, each 12 inches. Double each thread over-2 threads leading to alternated groupings, directly under first 5 square knots (see diagram a). With each group of 4 threads, make 10 knots to form a chain.
Remove macramé from working surface and position ring in the center over paper-weight. Holding macramé in position, turn paper-weight over and pin end of each group of knots to paper base. Cut a 48 inch length and double it. Lay the doubled length in a circle ¼ inch in from edge and knot each thread over this leader. Knot 3 rows of DHHs in all (see diagram b). Cut felt into circle 2½ inches in diameter, position over ends and glue in place.

Paper-weight II, yellow and brown
You will need
Paper-weight 2¾in diameter, ¾in deep
10 small wooden beads

How to make the paper-weight
Glue paper to base as for paper-weight I.
Cut 20 lengths each 28 inches and attach to plastic ring.
Divide into groups of 4 threads and make the first half of a square knot 18 times to form a spiral.

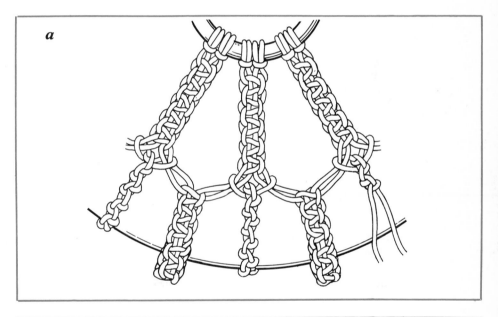

a

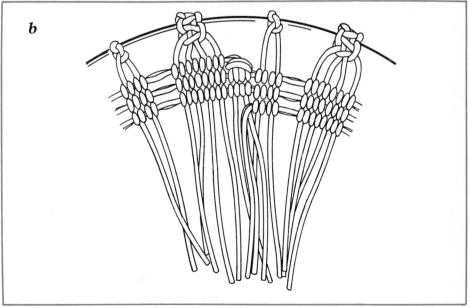

b

50

This hassock combines the effects of suede and macramé. It is an unusual idea and would look equally effective done in a different color suede or even in leather.

Cut 10 lengths each 14 inches, double and pin top loop in position between spirals. Using these new lengths as cores, and 2 cords from either side as working cords make the first half of a square knot 6 times to form a spiral.
Thread a bead onto each core and secure with one square knot.
Complete as for base of paper-weight I (see diagram b).

Paper-weight III, green and pink
You will need
Paper-weight 2¾in diameter, ⅜in deep
8 small wooden beads

How to make the paper-weight
Glue the felt to base of paper-weight.
Cut 20 lengths each 28 inches, double and attach ring.
Divide into groups of 5 threads and using center thread as core, with 2 threads on either side as working threads, make 3 square knots.
Thread bead onto core and secure with one square knot directly under bead.
Pin single core threads one inch below each square knot.
Using the 4 threads between the secured threads, make 8 square knots beginning ½ inch below bead.
Complete as for paper-weight I (see diagram b).

26 Hanging lampshade

N.B. The lampshade has 8 panels. There are 3 patterns to choose from, so either take 2 and work them alternately, around the shade, or take 3 and choose your favorite 2 to finish off with.

You will need (panels I, II, III)
White cotton cord
Lampshade frame, nylon coated with 8 panels

Measurements
Top diameter, 18in
Bottom diameter, 21½in
Depth, 9¾in excluding fringe
Fringe, 1½in

How to make panel I (see opposite)
[1]Cut lengths each 96 inches, double and attach to the frame in units of 20 per panel. Attach a doubled length on the vertical struts. Using a separate thread as a leader, knot one row of horizontal DHHs.[1] Take the 19th thread along and using it as a leader work double diagonal DHHs to the left.
Using the next thread not yet worked as a

leader, knot double diagonal DHHs to the right. These rows should form the top half of a diamond.
Take the 4 center threads and make a square knot. Continue working alternating square knots for the next 9 rows expanding the pattern at each row to form the first half of the diamond. Continue working rows of alternating square knots down to the base of the diamond. There should be 17 rows of square knots in all, the 9th row falling in the middle. Using the 2 outer threads on each side as leaders, knot double diagonal DHHs to right and left so that the diamond shape is completed.
[2]Using the 2 threads attached to the vertical strut, make 3 knots to form a DHH chain to the left and 3 to the right, until you reach the bottom.[2] DHH all the ends over the frame and trim tassels to the desired length.

You will need (panel II)
Nylon coated ring 5in diameter

How to make panel II (see page 84)
Repeat from [1] to [1] as in pattern II.
Make a braid on each side of the panel on 8 threads. *Knot a vertical knot from left to right, taking thread one over threads 2 and 3. Take thread 5 over thread 4 and make a vertical knot from right to left over threads 2 and 3. Take thread 8 and make a vertical knot from right to left over threads 6 and 7. Take thread 4 and make a vertical knot from left to right over threads 6 and 7.* Repeat from * to * 14 times alternating threads 4 and 5 so that the braid is linked.
Take the ring and place it so that it is in the middle of the panel (see photograph). DHH the remaining 24 threads onto the ring. Using the 13th thread as a leader work double diagonal DHHs to the left. Repeat this to the right using the next thread along as a leader. Weave the doubled threads in and out to form a criss-cross pattern and then complete diamond shape by knotting double diagonal DHH to the left and right (see diagram). Using a separate thread as a leader knot double horizontal DHH with the 2nd row over the base of the frame. Repeat from [2] to [2] as in pattern I. DHH these ends over the base of the frame and trim tassels.

How to make panel III (see page 85)
Repeat from [1] to [1] as in pattern I.
Divide the threads into groups of 10. Using thread 5 as a leader DHH diagonally to the left and then taking thread 6 as a leader DHH diagonally to the right. Make a square knot with these 10 threads. Complete the diamond. Continue across panel until 4 diamonds plus square knots have been completed. In the next row make 4 diamond shapes again but work 4 alternating square knots inside each shape. Repeat from * to *.
Repeat from [2] to [2] as in pattern 1, DHH all the ends onto the base of the frame and trim tassels to length required.

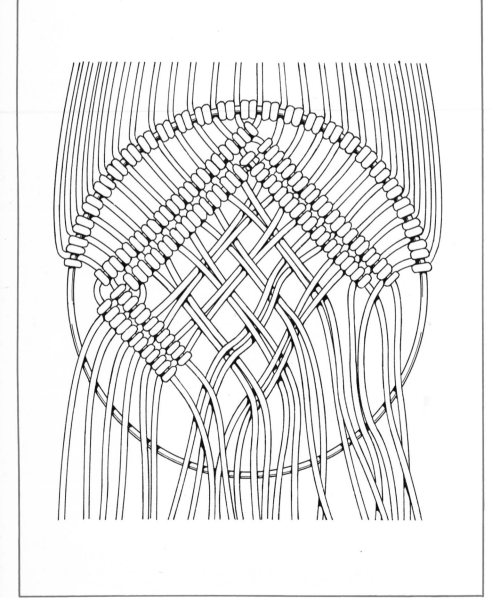

Weaving and working double diagonal DHHs

Panel I

Panel II

Panel III

27 Glasses case

You will need
50yds thin rattail cord or Tempo Nova rayon cord or 10/5 linen
6in square of felt
Matching thread

Measurements
5½in by 3in, excluding fringe
Fringe, 4½in

How to make the case
Cut 9 lengths each 72 inches, one length of 84 inches and a foundation thread about 6 inches. Attach the 9 threads doubled to the foundation thread. Fold the 84 inch length so that one end is 36 inches and the other 48 inches, and attach it to the right-hand side of the cord, so that the longest thread is the outer one. Use this thread as leader for horizontal DHHs throughout.
Knot 2 rows of horizontal DHHs.
*Divide the threads into groups of 4 and make 2 square knots on each group.
Knot double horizontal DHHs. Divide the threads into groups of 10 and knot 2 rows diagonal DHH to form a cross on each group. Knot double horizontal DHH.*
Repeat from * to *.
Divide the threads into groups of 4 and make 3 square knots on the first and last groups, 5 on the center group and 4 on the remaining 2 groups. Knot 2 rows of horizontal DHHs, following the line of the square knots.
Make a 2nd side the same.

To finish
Sew in the ends of the foundation thread.
Make a lining from the felt 5 inches by 5 inches. Fold in half lengthwise and overcast the side and lower edges together.
Place the macramé pieces wrong sides together, slip the lining between them and overcast macramé side edges. Catch stitch across between the bottom 2 rows of horizontal DHHs, through all thicknesses. Slip stitch lining in place around top edge.
Trim fringe to 4½ inches.

28 Covered lemonade jar

You will need
65 yds of thick polypropylene twine
32 medium ceramic beads
One glass jar
13yds fine String (stopper)
16 medium ceramic beads (stopper)

Measurements
Diameter at widest point, 8in
Height, 12in
Capacity ½ gal

How to make the cover
Cut a foundation thread 48 inches and make a small loop at one end.
Cut 13 lengths each 96 inches and attach on the loop. Pass one end of the foundation thread through the loop, place it around the neck of the jar and tighten.
Cut one more length 96 inches and attach it to the foundation thread to conceal the join.
Using the foundation thread as a leader, knot one row of horizontal DHHs around the top half of the jar. Leaving the leader, divide the threads into groups of 4 and make 7 square knots on each group, carrying leader down within the core of the nearest group of knots.
Cut 8 lengths each 72 inches. Knot one row of horizontal DHHs attaching one doubled 72 inch length between each group of square knots just made, plus one at the end so that the final number of threads is divisible by 4. Pass a bead onto each alternate thread and knot another row of horizontal DHHs. Divide the threads into groups of 4, so that each group is alternate to the previous square knots. Make the first half of a square knot 7 times on each group to form a spiral. Carry the leader down within the core of the nearest group of half knots.
Knot another row of horizontal DHHs, passing a bead onto the leader thread between each group of half square knots. Make an overhand knot on the leader thread, cut and conceal behind the work. Make alternating square knots over the rest of the bottle ¾ inch apart from one another.

To finish
Using one of the longer threads as a leader, knot 2 rows of horizontal DHHs around the base of the jar. The 2nd row should form a tight circle a fraction below the base, holding the work firmly in place. Trim ends to about ½ inch and glue to the base of the jar.

Covering the stopper
Cut a foundation thread 60 inches, which will also be used as a leader for horizontal DHHs. Cut 10 lengths each 24 inches.
Make a slip knot at one end of the foundation thread, double and attach to the 24 inch lengths. Pull the other end of the foundation thread through the slip knot and tighten. Pin this circle to working surface.
Divide threads into groups of 4, and pass a bead onto the 2 center threads. Make a square knot under each bead with 4 threads. Bring the leader (the foundation thread) down between the beads. Cut 10 lengths each 15 inches. Make a circle of horizontal DHHs, attaching 2 double threads between each square knot just made. Repeat from * to * once.
Remove macramé from working surface. Push stopper into jar and fit work over stopper. Hold the jar between the knees, and knot 2 rows of tight horizontal DHHs around the cork. Divide the threads into groups of 2 and make an overhand knot on each group. Trim.

29 Mobile

You will need
3 100yd balls plastic string or
3 100yd synthetic raffia (raffene)
2 wire coat hangers
2 embroidery hoops, 6in and 8in in diameter
Shells
Beads
Glue

How to prepare the hoop
Separate each part of embroidery hoops. Remove the tension screws from the outer hoops and flatten or clip off projecting parts. Tie the open ends together with fine wire or thread. Paint each inner and outer hoop with latex paint. Drill 2 small holes at opposite points in one of the 6 inch hoops and insert another length of wire at right angles to the first length, so that the hoop is now divided into 4 quarters. Glue the lengths of wire in place. Paint wires with latex paint. Repeat this on other part of the 6 inch hoop.

How to make the mobile
Upper section
Cut 40 lengths each 50 inches. Place one of the smaller wired hoops in a clamp or wedge it between your knees. Double one of the lengths so that one end is 13 inches and the other end is 37 inches. Hold the doubled end behind the hoop keeping the 13 inch length on the left.
Attach the length to the hoop with DHH knots as follows: take 37 inch length from back to front of hoop, over top and behind it and through loop of string at the bottom of the hoop (see diagram a). Repeat this.
Knot another 2 DHH knots with the 13 inch length (see diagram b). Knot another length in the same way only having the shorter length on the right and the longer on the left. There should now be 4 lengths with 2 shorter ones in the middle. Attach each length in the same way so that there are 5 pairs in each quarter of the hoop. There should now be 20 groups each consisting of 4 threads.
Make 9 square knots on each group.
How to attach one of the larger hoops
Take the 2 center threads from each group behind the larger hoop and the 2 outer threads in front of it (see diagram c). Make a square knot with all 4 threads directly underneath the hoop. Make square knots for 3 inches on each group. *Take the 2 center threads from each group and push them through from the front to the back of the larger hoop on each adjacent group to the right. The threads should be pushed through the spaces made for the purpose when attaching the larger hoop (see diagram c).* Bring these threads to the front of the hoop and make a square knot with all 4 threads to secure. Dab with glue and then cut ends.
This will form a series of spirals around the 2nd hoop in the mobile.
Middle section
From this point, work with the mobile hanging freely by a length of thread attached to wires of the upper hoop.
Cut 40 lengths each 156 inches, and attach 2 double lengths to the larger hoop in between each spiral with the knot to the inside of the ring. Make one square on each group of 4 threads. Make 4 more rows of alternating square knots approximately ½ inch apart. In the 6th row work 4 alternating square knots, skip the next square knot and make 4 more alternating square knots. Continue in this way all around the mobile.
In the 7th row make 3 alternating square knots under each group of 4 square knots, leaving out

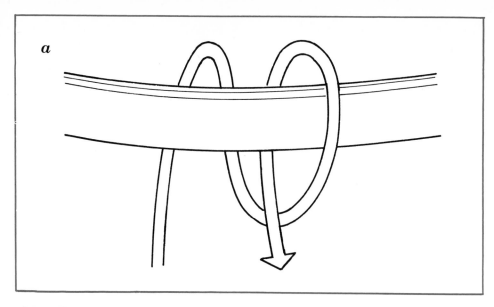

a

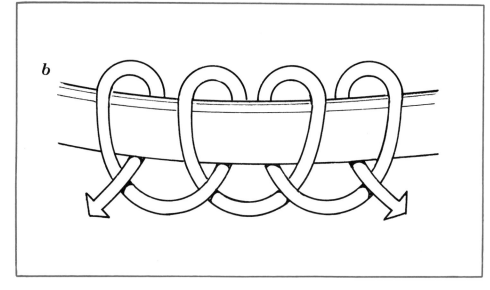

b

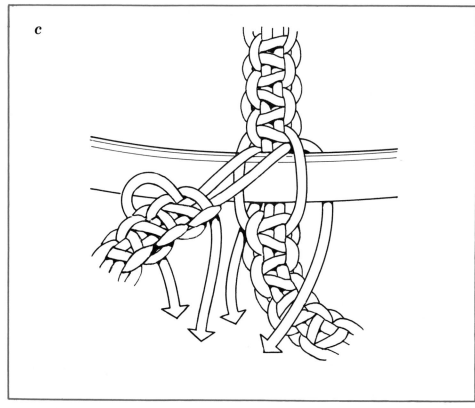

c

2 threads at each side of each group.

Make 2 alternating square knots in the 8th row in the same way as described for the 7th row. There will now be 8 threads only in each group. Make 8 rows of alternating square knots in each group, having one knot only on next and every alternate row.

Crossed bars

There will be a group of 12 threads in between each group of alternating square knots. Working from the left take the first 4 threads and make a series of collecting knots with thread 4 (see page 94) so that the threads are wrapped together for 1½ inches. Repeat with the next 2 groups of threads.

Using threads 1, 2, 11 and 12 make a square knot with threads 3 to 10 as a core. Continue making collecting knots with each group of 4 threads as before for a further 2 inches.

Leave these 12 threads hanging.

Work with each group of 12 threads in the same way.

Return to 4 groups of alternating square knots. Make 2 more rows of alternating knots in each group, increasing to 3 knots in the next row, 4 knots in the row after by using free threads on either side of the group. Now make 4 more rows of alternating square knots on all threads.

Lower section

Attach 2nd larger hoop in the same way as for the first small hoop. On each group of 4 threads knot 2 horizontal DHH knots on the left of the group with threads 1 and 2 over the hoop. Knot 2 horizontal DHH knots on the right with threads 3 and 4.

Make 3 single alternating knotted chains (6 knots) with 2 pairs of threads in each group. In each group of 4 threads make 9 square knots and then divide the groups in half and make 3 more single alternating knotted chains.

Take threads 3 and 4 of each group with threads 1 and 2 of adjacent group to form new groups of 4 threads. Take the 2 center threads to the back of the 2nd small hoop and bring the 2 outer threads around to the front of the hoop.

Make a square knot underneath with 4 threads and continue to make 4 inches of square knots. Repeat from * to * to form spirals. Make square knots on the groups of 4 threads for 3 inches.

To decorate the mobile

Shells with holes bored into them and green beads are strung at irregular intervals on separate lengths of string which are fastened between the wires in the 2 smaller hoops. Other decorations such as artificial flowers, cork bottle tops etc., can be used.

To finish

Tie all the threads together in the center of the mobile with 2 or 3 collecting knots (see page 94). Tie threads again about one inch lower down with 3 more collecting knots.

Decorate the head of the tassel by Turk's head wrapping (see page 37) or if preferred by wrapping with separate length of string. Secure ends with glue.

Trim hanging ends to a length of 5 inches.

30 Teheran pattern pillow

You will need
14oz skein each of white, light blue and dark blue in knitting yarn
½yd matching cotton lining
Pillowform 16in by 12in

Measurements
16in by 12in

How to make the pillow
Cut 24 lengths of white each 96 inches, 12 lengths light blue each 168 inches, 12 lengths dark blue each 168 inches and one foundation thread and 2 leaders each 15 inches.
Attach doubled threads on foundation in the following order: *2 white, one light blue, 2 dark blue, one light blue, 2 white, repeat from * 5 times more.
Knot one row of horizontal DHH, using separate leader across all threads. Divide threads into groups of 16 and using 2nd thread from the left as leader, DHH diagonally to the left across the next thread. Using the 4th thread as leader, DHH diagonally to the left across the next 2 threads. Take the 4 white threads and use them each in turn as leader, DHH diagonally across the 2·light blue and 2 dark blue threads to the right. Knot the other half of the group to correspond, reversing the direction of the diagonals. Knot across all the groups in this way.
Using the 4 light blue threads as core, make a square knot with the 2 dark blue threads on each side. Make a square knot in this way between each group. At the sides make half a knotted chain. On each group of 8 white threads, counting from the left, use the first thread as leader and DHH diagonally to the right over the 2nd thread. Using the 3rd thread as leader, DHH diagonally to the right over the 4th thread. Using the 5th and 6th threads together as one leader, DHH diagonally to the left over the next 4 threads.
Counting from the left again, use the 3rd thread as leader and DHH diagonally to the right over the 4th thread. Using the 5th thread as leader, DHH diagonally to the right over the 6th thread. Using the 2nd right-hand pair together as one leader, DHH diagonally to the left over the next 4 threads. Counting from the left again, use the 5th thread as leader, DHH diagonally to the right over the 6th thread. Using the 7th thread as leader, DHH diagonally to the right over the 8th thread. DHH the 4 white threads lying to the right each in turn diagonally to the right and the 4 white threads lying to the left over the colored threads.
Continue for 12½ rows of diamonds, reversing the colors of the square knots between the groups on each row.
Knot one row horizontal DHHs across all threads, using separate thread as leader.

To finish
Make matching lining and insert pillow form. Stitch macramé to front of pad.
Using dark blue, make a square knot braid long enough to go all around pillow. Stitch in place.

31 Placemat and napkin ring

You will need
140yds each of blue and green
Lily fine nylon macramé cord

Measurements
Mat. 19in by 11in.
Napkin ring. 7in round
Width, 1in

How to make the mat
Cut 16 lengths blue each 120 inches, one length blue 60 inches, 19 lengths green each 120 inches and one length green 60 inches. Cut 33 lengths blue each 60 inches and 39 lengths green each 60 inches. Pin the threads to the working surface 4 inches from the end, placing them in 9 groups of 8 threads each, positioning the groups 1¼ inches apart and with the following color sequence: 1st group all blue; 2nd group 2 blue (one green, one blue) 3 times; 3rd group (one green, one blue) 3 times, 2 green; 4th, 5th and 6th groups all green; 7th group 3 green, one blue (one green, one blue) twice; 8th group (one green, one blue) twice, 4 blue; 9th group all blue.
Make rows of alternating square knots for 14 inches. N.B. it is important to tie all the square knots in the same sequence so that it always faces in the same direction.
Using a length of blue thread, tie a constrictor knot (see diagram) around each group of 8 threads and trim ends to 3½ inches from the knot.
Using a length of green thread, tie a constrictor knot ¾ inch below each blue knot and trim to match the blue ends. Slacken 2 threads on either side of each group between the 2 knots to make loops. Trim all ends to one inch below the green knot and glue ends to prevent fraying.

How to make the napkin ring
Cut 3 lengths blue each 48 inches and one length green 48 inches.
Place 2 pins in working surface and loop threads evenly around them and arranging the sequence to have the left-hand group 2 blue, one green and one blue and the right-hand group to have one blue, one green and 2 blue.
Knot in rows of alternating square knots for 5 inches. Draw the ends through the starting loop and double the ends over.
Using a length of blue thread tie a constrictor knot around all 16 threads.
Tie a green constrictor knot directly below the blue one. Trim all ends to one inch and glue ends to prevent fraying.

Constrictor knot

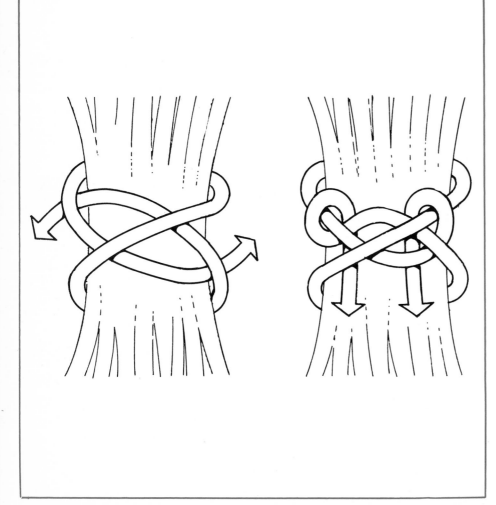

32 Guitar strap

You will need
110yds rayon cord or thin rattail in brown
55yds rayon cord or thin rattail in apricot
33 small wooden beads

Measurements
Length, 46½in
Width, 3in
Tie ends, 18in
Tassel, 3in
Fringe, 4in

How to make the strap
Cut 2 apricot lengths each 480 inches, 4 brown lengths each 600 inches, 2 brown lengths each 108 inches and one brown foundation thread about 6 inches.
Attach the lengths onto the foundation thread from the left in the following order: one 108 inch length, 2 600 inch lengths, 2 480 inch lengths, 2 600 inch lengths and one 108 inch length. Make 2 square knots on the 4 apricot threads.
Counting from the left, use the 13th thread as a leader and DHH diagonally to the left over the next 4 threads. Using the 14th thread as a leader, DHH diagonally to the left over the next 4 threads. Using the 4th thread as leader, DHH diagonally to the right over the next 4 threads. Using the 3rd thread as a leader, DHH diagonally to the right over the next 4 threads.
**Using the 3rd thread DHH vertically once over the 2nd thread and once over the first thread. Using the 4th thread, cord vertically once over the 3rd thread and once over the 2nd thread. Pin threads 1 and 2 to the left to make a ½ inch picot.
Using 2nd thread, DHH vertically over threads 3 and 4. Using the first thread, DHH vertically over each of threads 2 and 3. Knot the outer 4 threads on the right-hand edge to correspond.**
Using the 9th thread as leader, DHH diagonally to the left over the next 6 threads. Using the 10th thread as leader, DHH diagonally to the left over the next 6 threads.
Using the 10th thread as leader, DHH diagonally to the right across the next 4 threads. Using the 9th

thread as leader, DHH diagonally to the right across the next 4 threads.
Make a square knot with the center 4 threads. Place a bead onto the 2 core threads. Secure with one square knot.
Repeat from ** to ** once.***
Repeat from* to *** 28 times more, then from * to * once.
Using the center 4 threads, make one square knot.

Tie ends
Divide into 2 groups of 8 threads and work on each group separately. Using 8th thread as leader, DHH diagonally to the left across the next 3 threads. Using the 8th thread as leader, DHH diagonally to the left across the next 2 threads. Using the first thread as leader, DHH diagonally to the right across the next 7 threads. Using the first thread as leader, DHH diagonally to the right across the next 6 threads.
Using the 3rd thread as leader, DHH diagonally to the left across the next 2 threads. Using the 4th thread as leader, DHH diagonally to the left across the next 2 threads.
Using the 4 center threads, make one square knot. Repeat from the beginning of the tie ends twice more.
Using the 8th thread as leader, DHH diagonally to the left across the next 3 threads. Using the 8th thread as leader, DHH diagonally to the left across the next 2 threads.
Using the first thread as leader, DHH diagonally to the right across the next 3 threads. Using the first thread as leader, DHH diagonally to the right across the next 2 threads.
Take the center 4 threads and make one square knot. Using the 2nd thread as core, make one vertical DHH knot with the first thread. Knot the 7th and 8th threads to correspond. Using the center 4 threads as core, make a half vertical DHH knot alternately with right and then left 2 threads 6 times in all.
Leaving threads 1, 2, 7 and 8, use the remaining 4 threads to make double knotted chain for 12 inches. Leave a space of about ½ inch and tie ends to form a loop. Cut 20 lengths each 8 inches and double through the loop. Use 8 of these threads to make 3 rows of alternated square knots around the other threads, thus decorating the head of the tassel. Then use the same threads to work a collecting knot (see diagram on page 94), to secure tassel.
Make the 2nd tassel in the same way but thread a bead onto each of the 2 outer threads from each square knot stemming from the 3rd row of alternating knots. This will be 4 beads in all. Make a square knot under each bead to secure and tie a collecting knot underneath. Trim to the same length as the other tassel.

33 Lampshade

You will need
165yds nylon cord or 10/5 linen in apricot
110 yds nylon cord or 10/5 linen in coffee
186 medium beads in apricot
108 medium beads in fawn
Oval lampshade frame 7in deep
⅓yd 36in wide lampshade material for lining
Glue
Needle with a large eye
Beeswax

Measurements
Depth of lampshade including fringe 11in

How to make the lampshade
Cut 72 lengths of apricot each 54 inches, 6 lengths of coffee 84 inches and 36 lengths of coffee 66 inches. Double all the lengths and attach one of each of the 84 inch lengths on the 6 vertical struts on the frame. Attach the remaining lengths on each of the sections in the following order: one coffee, 4 apricot, 2 coffee, 4 apricot, 2 coffee, 4 apricot and one coffee. Make the first half of a square knot to make a spiral down each of the 6 vertical struts, until you come to the bottom. In order to finish, DHH the remaining threads around the ring at the bottom of the frame, and darn them into the back of the last 3 half square knots. Make all of the panels in the following way.
***Leaving the coffee threads at each end of the section, thread 2 apricot beads onto the 2 remaining groups of coffee. (If the ends of the lengths are well waxed they will pass easily through the beads.) Make 2 square knots onto the coffee threads at each end of the panel. Divide each group of apricot threads into 2 groups of 4 and make one square knot onto each group. Thread a fawn bead onto the 2 center threads of each group and make another square knot directly underneath.
Leaving the 2 threads on either side of each group, pass a fawn bead onto the 4 remaining center threads. Using the coffee threads as leaders, knot double diagonal DHHs over 4 threads to the bottom of each triangle.***
Gather all the coffee threads together and pass 2 apricot beads onto them. With the same threads make the first half of a square knot for 3 inches. Repeat from * to *.
Leaving the apricot threads behind each strut, take the center 4 threads from each of the remaining apricot groups and make a square knot 2½ inches down from the top of the frame. **Pass an apricot bead onto the 2 center threads, and make a square knot directly underneath.**
Divide all 8 threads into 2 groups of 4 and make a square knot on each. Repeat from ** to ** on each group. Take the 4 center threads and make a square knot. Repeat from ** to **.
Repeat from *** to *** reversing the pattern in order to begin with double diagonal DHHs. DHH each thread around the base of the frame. Using the coffee threads as leaders knot double diagonal DHHs over the apricot threads. Pass an apricot bead onto each group of coffee threads. Make a collecting knot with 2 threads (see page 94), on each apricot group. Trim tassels to 3 inches.

To finish
Make a paper pattern to fit inside the lampshade. Cut out the lampshade material allowing ¼ inch at each end for the join. Glue the join together. Stick the lining into the lampshade glueing at the upper and lower edges.

34/35 Cavandoli mats

Navy and white mat
You will need
4 4oz skeins of rug wool in navy
2 4oz skeins of rug wool in white

Measurements
Length, 23½in
Width, 11½in

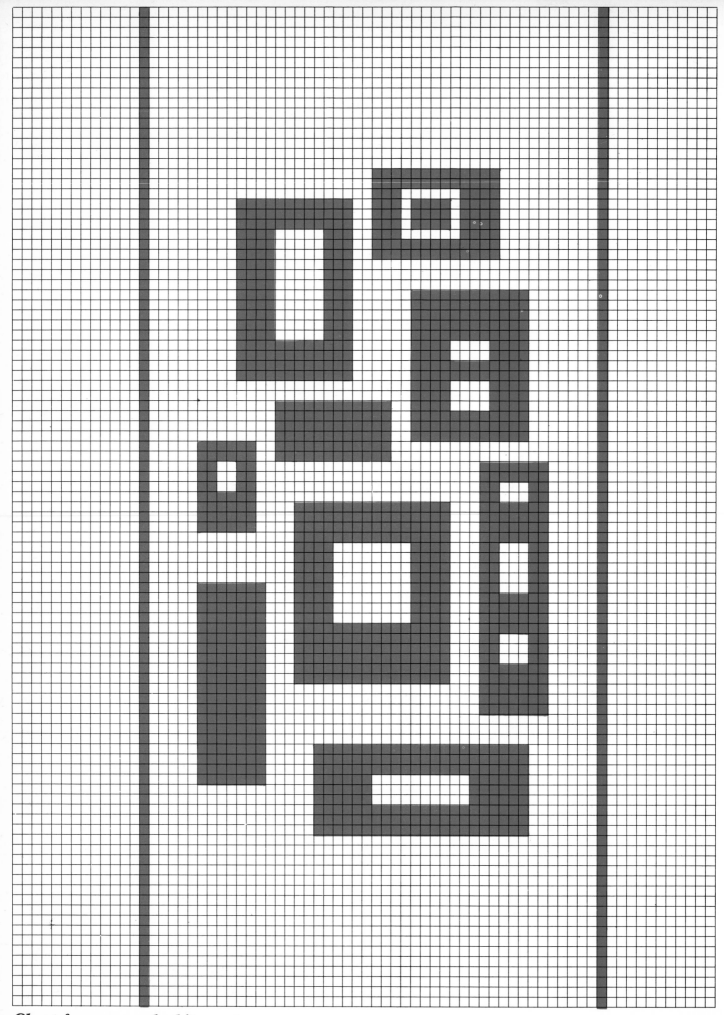

Chart for navy and white mat

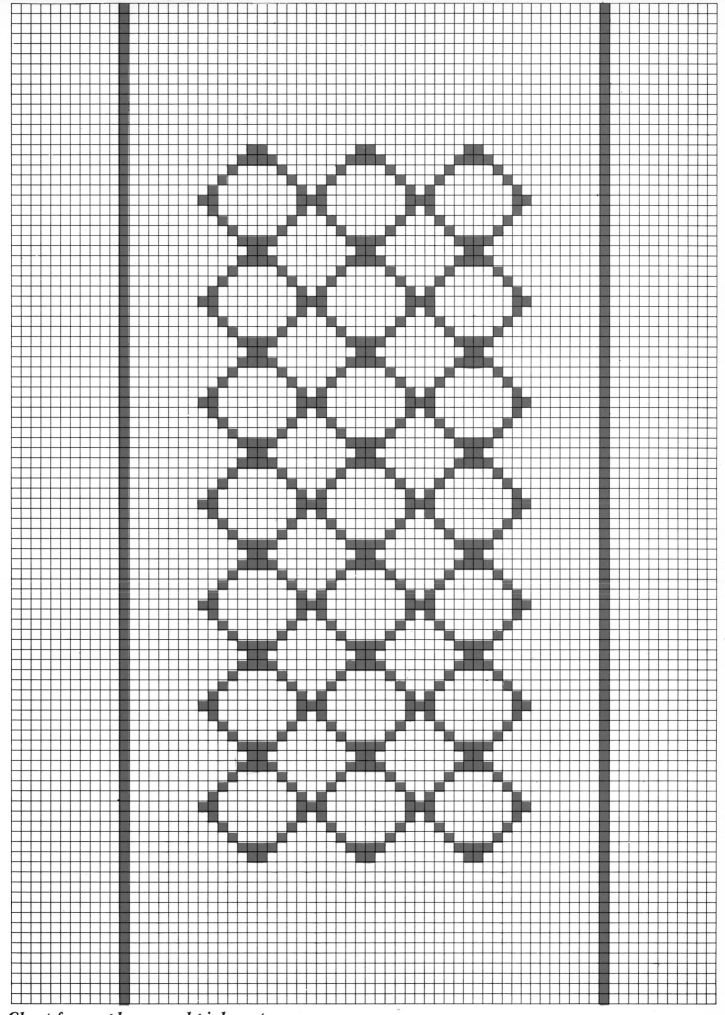

Chart for raspberry and pink mat

How to make the mat

The instructions for the Cavandoli technique are shown in the Crash Course at the back of the book on page 111. Work from the chart on page 90. Cut a foundation thread in navy 24 inches, and pin it to the working surface. There are 24 threads in navy to be attached in varying lengths.

The first and last threads are 168 inches. Fold them in half so that one end is 36 inches and the other end 132 inches. Attach them to the foundation thread so that the shortest threads are the first and last.

In the middle all the other threads are doubled and attached as follows: 2nd, 3rd and 4th threads, 264 inches; 5th, 6th and 7th threads, 216 inches; 8th, 9th and 10th threads, 240 inches; 11th to 19th threads, 216 inches; 20th and 21st threads, 240 inches; 22nd and 23rd threads, 264 inches. Make a ball of 1½ skeins of white wool, attach to left side of work and begin knotting horizontal DHHs. Picots should be made at the beginning and end of every row in white. The pattern begins at the 7th row. When following the pattern, put a piece of paper over the chart and move it down as the work progresses as it is easy to miss a row.

To finish

Sew in the ends of the foundation thread. Turn in all the other ends and sew them into the back, trim. If necessary, the ends can be stuck down with carpet tape.

Raspberry and pink mat
You will need

4 4oz skeins of rug wool in raspberry
3 2oz skeins of rug wool in pink

Measurements

Length, 23½in
Width, 12in

How to make the mat

The instructions for the Cavandoli technique are shown in the Crash Course at the back of the book on page 111. Work from the chart given on page 91. Cut a foundation thread in raspberry 24 inches and pin it to the working surface. There are 25 threads in raspberry to be attached in varying lengths.

The first and last threads are 168 inches. Fold them in half so that one end is 36 inches and the other end 132 inches. Attach them to the foundation thread so that the shortest threads are the first and last threads.

In the middle, all the other threads are doubled and attached as follows: 2nd to 5th threads, 264 inches; 6th thread, 240 inches; 7th thread, 216 inches; 8th to 11th thread, 240 inches; 12th thread, 264 inches; 13th thread, 261 inches, then in reverse order to the end.

Make a ball of 1½ skeins of pink wool (if this is too much to handle, use half and when thread finishes add in the next half at the side, sew it in at the back afterwards). Attach ball to left side of work and begin knotting horizontal DHHs. Picots should be made at the beginning and end of every row in pink. The pattern begins at the 7th row. Follow the chart exactly.

To finish

Sew in the ends of foundation thread. Turn in all ends and sew into the back, trim. If necessary the ends can be stuck down with carpet tape.

36 String lampshade

You will need

Lampshade frame, nylon coated with 6 panels
Ball of cotton string
24 wooden beads
Large-eyed needle
Lining

Measurements

Top diameter, 9in
Bottom diameter, 9½in
Depth, 6½in

How to make the lampshade

Cut 5 lengths each 86 inches, one length 186 inches and 72 lengths each 60 inches.

Attach the 86 inch lengths on the top of 5 of the vertical struts on the frame, one thread hanging on either side of the strut. Attach the 186 inch length on the top of the 6th vertical strut, making the left thread 43 inches and the right thread 143 inches. Using the strut as a core, make 23 square knots over each vertical strut.

Attach 12 of the 60 inch lengths onto each section, making the outer threads of each section 48 inches and the next thread in at each side 12 inches. The 10 center threads are doubled evenly.

The 2 opposite sections of the frame holding the ring support are both worked in the same way.

Divide the threads in these 2 sections into 6 groups of 4 and make 3 square knots on each group. Leaving the outer 2 threads at each side in each section, make a row of alternating square knots. Using the right-hand thread as a leader, knot one row of horizontal DHHs.

Using the same leader, knot a 2nd row of DHHs. Make a row of 6 square knots.

Make 5 more rows of alternating square knots, leaving one knot per row so that the pattern forms a triangle.

Using the outer threads as leaders, knot double diagonal DHHs in line with the edge of the alternating square knots.

Using the outer 4 threads at each side, make 4 square knots. Using the next 4 threads on either side make 2 square knots and on each of the 2 remaining groups of 4 threads make one square knot.

Leaving the outer threads at each side and the center 4 threads, make 3 square knots on each of the remaining 4 groups of 4 threads. Make one square knot on the center 4 threads.

On the 4 remaining sections of the frame, make 3 square knots on all 6 groups of 4 threads. Leaving the outer 2 threads at each side, make 2 square knots on the remaining 5 groups.

Place a bead on the 2nd thread at each side.

Using the needle, pull the remaining outer threads through the 5th square knot on the frame.

Make 9 rows of 2 alternate square knots *at the same time* repeating from ** to ** on every alternate row and repeating from * to * on every 4th row.

To finish

Using the remainder of the 143 inch length which was used on one of the vertical struts as leader, pull each remaining length tightly over the bottom of the frame and knot 2 rows of horizontal DHHs.

Make 2 square knots on every group of 4 threads all around and tie an overhand knot on each group. Trim the ends to measure 2 inches from the overhand knot.

A lining can be sewn loosely onto the inside of the lampshade so that the macramé can be seen more clearly.

37 Wall hanging

You will need

6 4oz skeins rug wool
One 18in length brass tubing and
2 curtain rod finials
or
One 24in length bamboo or wooden dowel

Measurements

Length, 36in including fringe
Width, 24in

How to make the hanging

Cut 34 lengths each 288 inches, one length 408 inches and one length 528 inches. All the work is done with double threads used as one thread to make the knots thicker and the pattern stand out boldly.

There are 8 double rows or horizontal DHHs which are worked by using the first or last doubled thread as a leader, taking it across and back. The first doubled thread is longer than all the others as it is used for vertical DHH knots.

Attach 36 doubled threads to the tubing making the first thread the longest and the last thread the 2nd longest. Secure with 2 rows of horizontal DHHs, using the right-hand outside doubled thread as leader and taking it across and back again. Divide threads into groups of 4 doubled threads. Make the first half of a square knot 10 times so that each cord forms a spiral, the first and every alternate ones twist once, every other alternate one twists twice.

Knot 2 rows of horizontal DHHs, using the first doubled thread as leader. Still using this thread, knot 2 rows (across and back once) of vertical DHH knots (to work vertical DHH knots hold the first thread behind the 2nd thread, knot 2 vertical DHH knots, then hold the first thread behind the 3rd thread and repeat, etc.

Knot 2 rows of horizontal DHHs using the first doubled thread as a leader. Divide the threads into groups of 4 doubled threads and make 7 rows of alternate square knots. Knot 2 rows of horizontal DHHs using the first doubled thread as a leader. Divide the threads into groups of 6 doubled threads and knot a double diagonal DHH cross in each group.

Knot 2 rows of horizontal DHHs using the first doubled thread as a leader. Divide the threads into groups of 3 doubled threads and make 3 square knots on each. Knot 2 rows of horizontal DHHs using the last doubled thread as leader. Divide threads into groups of 4 doubled threads. Using the right-hand doubled thread of each group, knot 3 vertical DHH knots. Divide threads again alternately into groups of 4 and repeat for 4 rows in this manner.

Knot 2 rows of horizontal DHHs using the last doubled thread as a leader.

Make 2 knotted chains on each pair of doubled threads right across the row, then knot 2 rows of horizontal DHHs using the last doubled thread as leader.

To finish

Cut off the threads at the required length of fringe and unravel the strands.

38 White pillow cover

You will need
110yds bulky sayelle yarn
One pillow form, 12in by 16in

Measurements
12in by 16in

How to make the pillow cover
Cut 18 lengths each 192 inches, one foundation thread 18 inches and one separate leader 18 inches long.
Pin foundation thread to working surface and attach doubled threads.
Divide threads into groups of 4, make 2 square knots on each group.
Make a braid of 3 vertical DHH knots with first and last pairs of threads. Divide remaining threads into groups of 4 and make 2 square knots on each group. Working the vertical braid in this way at outer edges on every alternate row throughout, make 3 more rows alternated square knots.
Using right-hand thread of 2 center threads as leader, DHH diagonally to the right across the next 3 threads. Using left-hand thread of 2 center threads, DHH diagonally to the left across next 3 threads. With all remaining threads make another row of alternated square knots. Continue the diagonals to right and left over a further 2 threads. Continue center diamond, DHH center right thread diagonally to left across 5 threads, center left thread diagonally to right across 4 threads, center right thread diagonally to left across 4 threads, center left thread diagonally to right across 3 threads, center right thread diagonally to left across 3 threads, center left thread diagonally to right across 2 threads, center right thread diagonally to left across 2 threads, center left thread diagonally to right across one thread, center

right thread diagonally to left across one thread.
Using outside threads of center diamond motif as leaders, DHH into center, crossing left leader over right leader at center.
With remaining threads work one more row alternated square knots.
Using the pair of threads next to center motif on either side as leaders each in turn, DHH diagonally into the center. DHH upper leader onto lower leader, then cross right leader over left leader. Make one row alternated square knots on remaining threads.
Make one row of 2 alternate square knots on remaining thread. Using the inner 2 threads of these remaining threads make 3 knots to form single chain.
Make one more row alternated square knots.
Thread each outside thread of the center motif once through the center knotted chain beside it.
Complete the 2nd half of pillow to correspond in reverse to the first half, ending with one row of horizontal DHHs with separate leader.
Knot pairs of threads with an overhand knot, pull firmly and trim ends.

To finish
Sew in ends of foundation thread and separate leader.
Attach work to front of pillow form.

39 Stool top

You will need
2 2 oz skeins each of dark green, light green, orange in rug wool (A, B, C in that order)

One inch thick foam rubber 13in by 11in
Lining fabric 29in by 13in
Matching thread

Measurements
14½in by 11½in excluding fringes
Fringes, 4in

How to make the stool top
Cut 5 lengths A each 144 inches, 5 lengths B each 144 inches, 12 lengths C each 102 inches and 2 separate C leaders each 24 inches. Pin doubled threads to working surface in following order:
*2 C threads, one B thread, one A thread. Repeat from * 4 more times, and then attach 2 C threads. 6 inches below pins introduce separate leader (see diagram).
Knot 2 rows of horizontal DHHs across all threads.
In each group of C except the group on the right-hand side of the work, use 4th thread as leader and DHH diagonally to the right across next 2 threads. Repeat with each 3rd C thread. In each group of C except the group on the left-hand side of the work, use first thread as leader and DHH diagonally to the left across next 2 threads. Repeat with each 2nd C thread. Make one square knot on each group of 4 C threads. Under each square knot use first C thread as leader to DHH diagonally to the left over the next 2 threads, repeat with the 2nd C thread, then use 4th thread as leader to DHH diagonally to the right over the next 2 threads and repeat with 3rd thread. On each group, using 2 B threads as core, make 2 square knots with A threads.
Using left-hand group of C, make 3 knots to form chain.
Repeat with the right-hand group.
On each of 6 C groups make one knot to form chain with the first and 2nd threads and then one knotted chain with the 3rd and 4th threads.
Using the 3rd thread as leader, DHH diagonally to the left across the next 2 threads. Repeat with

Threads for stool top pinned in place

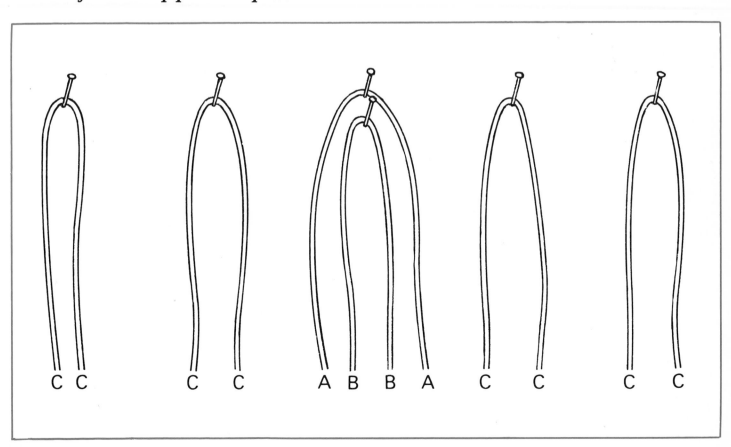

C   C   C   C   A   B   B   A   C   C   C   C

93

the 4th thread as leader. Make one knotted chain with the first and 2nd threads, and then one knotted chain with the 3rd and 4th threads.***
Repeat from ** to *** 4 times more, then from **to ** once.
Using 2nd separate leader, knot 2 rows horizontal DHHs across all threads.

To finish
Trim fringes to about 4 inches.
Make lining from fabric, allowing ½ inch seams.
Insert foam into lining and close seam.
Using a length of C, split it into separate strands and using 2 strands together, sew macramé to pillow.

40 *Pillow and pad for rocking chair*

You will need
Back pad. 2 2 oz skeins each of blue, cream, one 2oz skein of plum in rug wool
One piece of foam, 12in by 13in, 1in thick
Lining material, 26in by 15in
Seat pad. 3 2oz skeins each of blue, plum, 4 2oz skeins of cream in rug wool
One piece of foam, 18in by 18in, 2in thick
Lining material, 18in by 36in

Make in the same way as the Teheran pattern pillow

Measurements
Back pad. 13½in by 11in
Seat pad. 15½in by 15½in

How to make the back pad
Cut 12 lengths blue each 78 inches, 6 lengths plum each 104 inches and 6 lengths cream each 104 inches. Attach and work as for Persian pillow (see pattern 30), substituting blue for white, plum for light blue and cream for dark blue, making 5 rows alternating full diamonds with a half diamond at each end.

How to make the seat pad
Cut 16 lengths each 84 inches, 8 lengths plum each 114 inches and 8 lengths cream each 114 inches. Attach and work as for Persian pillow as given for back pad.

To finish
Edging
For the back pad cut a length of cream 55 inches to go around the pillow and a length 426 inches wound into a ball; for the seat pad cut a length 60 inches and another length 558 inches wound into a ball. Pin the end of the short length to the working surface and then pin the end of the longer length to the right of it. Knot vertical DHHs with the longer length over the shorter length, making a ¾ inch picot after every 3rd knot. Continue to the length of the circumference of the pillow. Sew the fringe to the outer edge of the macramé.
Tie
Cut 2 lengths 300 inches of cream. Lay them side by side. Secure one end and twist the other end clockwise until it is very tight. Double the threads

and twist counter-clockwise. Secure both ends in a collecting knot and trim tassel to required length.

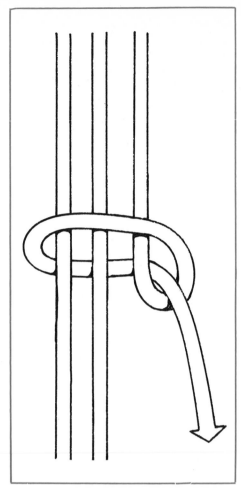

Collecting knot made over two threads

41 *Dog leash and Collar*

You will need
26yds cotton seine twine medium
22yds cotton seine twine medium (collar)
One metal dog leash fastener
One gold buckle, 1in by 1½in deep, with center spike (collar)
One gold D-ring (collar)
Glue

Measurements
Leash. Length, 30in excluding tassel
Width, ½in
Tassel, 7in
Collar. Length, 15in
Width, 1in

How to make the leash
Cut 2 lengths each 11 yards and one length 4 yards, double and attach to the ring of fastener with the short lengths in the center. Using these short lengths as a core make flat knots for 24 inches.

Divide the 6 threads into 2 groups of 3. Using the shorter thread in each group as a core make 6 inches of square knots on each group.
Make an overhand knot with all 6 threads. Cut tassel to 7 inches and fray out ends.

How to make the collar
Cut 2 lengths each 120 inches, 2 lengths each 60 inches and 2 lengths each 216 inches. Double them, attaching them across buckle bar in the following order: one 216 inch length, one 60 inch length, one 216 inch length, one 216 inch length, one 60 inch length and one 120 inch length, so that the spike comes between the 2 216 inch lengths in the center. Divide threads into 2 groups of 6, and using the 2 center threads as a core make 2 square knots on each group. The square knots on the left are made with the loop to the left (left threads over core threads first), and the square knots on the right are made with the loop to the right (right threads over core threads first).
Make an overhand knot with the 4 center threads (2 from each square knot). Divide threads into 2 groups of 6. Make one square knot with the loop to the left, and one square knot with the loop to the right.
Repeat from * to * until there are 11 overhand knots in the center.
In order to incorporate D-ring, loop the 4 center threads over the flat side of the D-ring before making the next 3 overhand knots.
Repeat from * to * until the collar measures 15 inches.

To finish
Make 2 square knots each over 6 threads. Make a square knot with 4 center threads. Turn in threads and sew in at the back. Cut and secure with a little clear glue.

For the bowl illustrated you will need
Polished twine
One curtain ring
Roll cellophane tape
5 rectangular glass beads
30 round beads

Measurements
To fit bowl 4in deep. 8in diameter
Length of suspension cords, 21in

How to make the braid
On the bowl illustrated there are 10 lengths of twine, each 120 inches.

Large candle jar
The threads are attached to a curtain ring which is taped to the center of the jar base. The shape is then enclosed in a pattern of square knots and beads. Cut a number of lengths of string divisible by 8, each 10 times the depth of the container and the diameter added together, plus 10 times the length of the suspension cord. Attach the doubled threads onto the ring in groups of 4 doubled threads. Tape the ring to the base. Tape each group of threads to the edge of the base.
Divide the threads into 2 groups of 4 threads each and make 5 square knots on each group. Thread an oval bead on the core threads of each group and make one square knot to hold in place. Using all 8 threads together of each group, make a square knot with 3 threads on each side and 2 core threads.
Thread a round bead onto the core threads of each group and make one square knot to secure. Divide each group into 2 groups of four threads, make one square knot on each group, pass the core threads through an oval bead, then make 5 square knots.

Tape the completed braids in place. Take each group of 4 threads to slope toward the group of 4 in the next group, to alternate the groupings. With each new group of 8 threads * make a square knot with 3 threads on either side of 2 core threads, pass the core threads through a small round bead, make another square knot to secure.* Divide the threads into groups of 4 and work 5 square knots on each group, thread an oval bead onto the core threads, make one square knot to secure. Alternate the groups to take them back to their original grouping, repeat from * to * within one inch of the top of the jar. Tape groups in place. Cut 4 lengths of thread each 10 times the circumference of the top of the jar. Double and attach onto a short holding cord. Work from * to * until braid fits jar top tightly.
Pass the ends through the attached threads at the beginning to make a circle and knot in pairs at the back of the work. Trim ends and glue.
Position this band round the top of the jar, over the threads already worked. Lightly glue in place. Continue on the original groups of 8 threads.
Using 4 core threads and 2 threads on each side, make 23 square knots. Make an overhand knot with each pair of side threads and trim.
Using the 4 remaining threads, make one square knot, thread a round bead onto center 2 threads, then make 23 square knots.
Taking all the threads together from the four groups, make one large overhand knot. Trim tassel.

For the jar illustrated you will need
Cotton seine twine
One curtain ring
32 small round beads
12 oval wooden beads
Cellophane tape
Candle

42 Hanging gardens

Hanging bowl
The threads are attached to a curtain ring which is taped to the center of the base of the bowl. The shape is then enclosed in a pattern of alternating square knots.
Cut an even number of lengths of string each 4 times the depth of the container, plus 5 times the length of the suspension cords.
Attach the doubled threads to the ring. Turn the container upside down and tape the ring and thread to the center of the base.
Take each pair of doubled threads and tape to the bowl at the edge of the base. Make 2 square knots. Using 2 threads from each square knot together with 2 threads from the next square knot, make 2 more square knots which will therefore be alternated with the first sets of knots.
Continue in alternating square knots to the rim of the bowl, taping the knots to keep them in place. Once the bowl is suspended, the knots will stay in place automatically and the tape can be removed. Divide the threads as before and with each pair of doubled threads, make 8 square knots. Thread a glass bead onto the 2 core threads, make 21 square knots, *thread on 2 small beads, make 2 square knots, repeat from * twice more, then make 5 square knots. Make an overhand knot with all 4 threads.
Taking all the suspension threads together, make a large overhand knot positioned 10 inches from the last square knot.

Measurements
To fit jar 7½in deep, 3in diameter
Length of suspension cords, 10in

How to make the braid
On the jar illustrated there are 16 lengths each 192 inches.
The two opposite groups have orange oval beads and the alternate opposite groups have yellow oval beads.
The repeat from * was worked once only to * to reach within one inch of the jar top.
For the band around the top of the jar, from * to * was worked 16 times.

Hanging plant pot
The threads are attached to a curtain ring which is placed inside the pot and the threads are taken through the hole in the base to the outside. The shape is then enclosed in a pattern of alternating square knots.
Cut an even number of threads each 4 times the depth of the pot plus 5 times the length of the suspension cords.
Insert the ring inside the pot and draw the threads through the hole to the outside.
Make square knots on each group of 4 threads until the edge of the base is reached. Tape in place.
Divide the threads into pairs and taking one pair from one group together with a pair from the next group, make 2 square knots on each group. Tape the knots in place.
Again taking 2 threads from one group together with 2 threads from the next group, make 2 square knots on each group.
Continue in this way, alternating the position of the knots, and work to the top of the pot.
With each group, make 8 square knots. Using a blunt-ended needle, thread the 2 center threads from front to back through the knot above the center of the first knot. Make a little blackberry ball. Make 2 square knots to secure.
Using the first half of the square knot only so that the braid twists, continue until spiral measures 4 inches. Pass all the threads of each group through a large glass bead.
Continue in half knots but using the previous core threads as outside threads and vice versa. Make another 4 inches of spiral braid. Make an overhand knot on each group.
Taking all threads from the 4 groups together, make a large overhand knot 7 inches above the small overhand knots. Trim the tassel.

For the pot illustrated you will need
Twine
One curtain ring
Cellophane tape
4 large rectangular glass beads

Measurements
To fit pot 5½in deep, 6in top diameter
Length of suspension cords, 18in

How to make the braid
On the pot illustrated there are 8 threads, each 120 inches.

Jar with lip
The jar is held just under the lip by one braid of single knotted chain and hung from 3 suspension cords.
Cut one length of twine 8 times the circumference of the jar, and 2 lengths each 5 times the length of the suspension cords.
Using the long piece of twine, fold it in half and pin to a secure base. Using the right-hand thread as core, knot the left-hand thread around it once, leaving a small loop at the top, then using the left-hand thread as core, knot the right-hand thread around it. This is called a single knotted chain.

Continue in this way for the circumference of the jar less one inch. Fit the braid around the jar, pass the ends of the string through the loop at the beginning and pull the braid tight.
Continue with single knotted chain until a further 12 inches have been worked.
Using the crochet hook, pull each of the other 2 lengths through the knotted chain around the jar, one on each side of the first suspension chain, a third of the way around the jar. Pull the ends even and make a single knotted chain for 12 inches. Taking all 6 threads together, make one large overhand knot. Trim ends.

For the jar illustrated you will need
Polished twine
One crochet hook

Measurements
To fit jar 4½in deep
Length of suspension cords, 12in

How to make the braid
For the jar illustrated there are one 72 inch length and 2 60 inch lengths.

43 Curtain hanging

You will need
20 4oz skeins rug wool
70yds Lilyfine nylon macramé cord
½in wooden dowel 35in long
One 5in diameter ring
One 7in diameter ring
One 16in diameter ring
123 bamboo curtain beads

Measurements
27in by 67in

How to make the hanging
Cut 60 lengths each 15 yards and 8 lengths each 128 inches.
Attach the longer lengths onto the dowel.
Using the left-hand thread as leader, DHH horizontally across all threads. Counting from the left, use threads 21 to 32. Divide them into 3 groups of 4 threads each and make 2 square knots on each group, 7 inches below horizontal DHHs.
Next, use threads 17 to 32 and divide into 4 groups of 4 threads each. On the left-hand group make 2 square knots, on the other group make one knot. Make a 3rd row of alternated square knots, adding one group to each side. Continue in rows of alternating square knots worked to the shape of a circle, making the widest point where the outer left-hand group is added in and leaving the center 17 threads free.
Before working the lower half of the circle, place a bead on each of these free threads, tying an overhand knot under each bead to hold it in the required position. On threads 69 to 72 make the first half of a square knot to form a spiral, beginning 4½ inches from horizontal DHHs and continuing for 8 inches.
On next group of 4 threads make a second spiral, 3 inches below the horizontal DHHs for 8 inches. Make 8 more spirals in this way as follows: 6 inches down for 8 inches, one inch down for 11½ inches, 9½ inches down for 5½ inches, 5 inches down for 8 inches, 8 inches down for 7 inches, 4 inches down for 7 inches, 2½ inches down for 7 inches, 6½ inches

down for 4 inches.
DHH the threads of the 3rd spiral onto the largest ring.
Attach 2 lengths nylon cord doubled as one to each side of the 3rd spiral and 2 doubled pairs between the 2nd and 3rd threads of the 3rd spiral. DHH on 33 threads to the left and 37 to the right of the 3rd spiral, introducing a pair of nylon cords as one between 2nd and 3rd threads of 6th spiral.
Using threads 1 to 40, work 11 spirals as before, as follows: 18 inches down for 5 inches, 21 inches down for 3 inches, 19 inches down for 5 inches, 21 inches down for 2 inches, 18 inches down for 9 inches, 23 inches down for 7 inches, 20 inches down for 14 inches, 22 inches down for 8 inches, 20½ inches for 7 inches, 17½ inches for 15½ inches, 24 inches down for 5 inches and first linking one thread to the ring. Under the first 4 spirals make 3 alternated spirals, the first for 4½ inches, the 2nd for 6½ inches and the 3rd for 13 inches. Under the first 2 of these make 2 further alternated spirals, the first for 2½ inches, the 2nd for 4½ inches. Using the 2 threads to the left of the 13 inch spiral and 2 threads from the spiral, make a one inch spiral.
DHH threads 15 to 55 onto the 7 inch ring, placing it directly below the 14 and 15½ inch spirals.
Make the center braid of the large ring on threads from 3rd spiral in nylon cord, using cord double throughout. Knot 3 rows diagonal DHHs into the center and link with a blackberry ball. Knot 3 rows diagonal DHHs out again. Repeat this twice more then knot 3 rows diagonal DHHs into the center again. DHH onto lower part of ring. On the 3 groups of 4 threads to the left of the center braid, make one square knot on each group. Make 2 rows alternated square knots under this*. Thread a bead onto the 4th, 5th, 8th and 9th threads and secure with one square knot under each pair of beads. Make one square knot on the outer 4 threads of this section and thread a bead onto the center 2 threads. Secure with one square knot under the pair of beads then make a row of 2 alternated square knots, then a row of 3 alternated square knots.* Repeat from * to * then make 2 rows more alternated square knots. DHH onto lower part of ring.
On next groups of 4 threads to the left of this, make one square knot on each group. Using the right-hand group as leaders each in turn, knot 4 rows of diagonal DHH to the left across the left-hand group. Divide threads into 2 groups of 4 and make one square knot on each group. Make a diagonal cross. Repeat this 3 times, leaving out lower half of last cross. DHH onto lower part of ring.
On the 8 threads to the left of this work 11 rows alternated square knots, beginning with a single square knot on center 4 threads. DHH onto lower part of ring.
On the last group of threads work a zig-zag of diagonal DHHs at the same time knotting over the side of the ring to cover it completely.
On the group of 8 threads to the right of the center braid, work a spiral using the left-hand thread over the other 7 threads. After 4½ inches, divide into 2 spirals for 4 inches, work single spiral for 2 inches, 2 spirals for 3 inches and finish with single spiral before knotting DHHs onto lower part of ring.
Using the nylon cord double, on the next group of 6 threads work diagonal DHHs to right and left for the required length. DHH onto the lower part of the ring.
On the next group of 4 threads work double knotted chain for 5 inches, 2 braids of single knotted chain for 3 inches and complete to the required length with double knotted chain. DHH onto the ring.
On the next group of 4 threads make a spiral for 5 inches, square knot braid with picots after every 3rd knot for 4½ inches and complete to the required length with a spiral. DHH onto ring.

Detail of the hanging

On the next group of 4 threads make a square knot braid with picots after every 3rd knot for the required length. DHH onto ring.

On the next group of 8 threads knot 3 rows of diagonal DHHs to the right.
Using the 5th thread as leader, DHH diagonally to the left across the next 4 threads. Knot 2 more rows under this one. Thread a bead onto each of the 3 remaining threads. Knot 2 rows diagonal DHHs to the right across all threads. Repeat the diagonal DHHs to the left as before, and thread a bead onto each of the next 2 threads. DHH onto the ring. Complete the last group of threads to correspond with the left-hand group.
Divide the right-hand 24 threads into 6 groups of 4 threads and work spirals from the left-hand group as follows: first spiral, from the ring for 14 inches; 2nd, from 3 inches below ring for 7½ inches; 3rd, from the ring for 17 inches; 4th, from the ring for 23 inches; 5th, from the ring for 16 inches; link the last group into the ring about half-way down the side edge and make a spiral for 14 inches.
Skip 8 threads to the left of these spirals, then DHH the next 30 threads onto the 5 inch ring. Make one square knot on each group of nylon threads and one knotted chain on the 2 wool threads between the 2 groups. *Thread a bead on each of the knotting threads of the square knots and a bead on one of the wool threads. Make a square knot and knotted chain on the same threads as before.* Repeat from * to * once more. On the remaining threads at either side, make alternating square knots with 2 beads on the right-hand group and one bead in the center of the left-hand group. DHH all threads onto the lower half of the ring.
On the left-hand group of 4 threads on the ring, make a spiral for 5 inches. On the next group of 4 threads to the left, make a spiral from 13 inches below the large ring for 5 inches. On the next group make a spiral from 9 inches below the large ring for 11 inches. On the next group make a spiral from 15 inches below the large ring for 6 inches. From the first group from the next ring, make a spiral 4 inches from the ring for 4 inches. On the next group make a spiral from the ring for 11 inches. On the last 2 threads on this ring with 2 threads from the next group to the left, make a spiral for 2 inches.
Using the left-hand thread as leader, DHH horizontally, across all threads. Make overhand knots and place beads at random on the fringe. Trim to about 18 inches. Double 4 of the shorter lengths and work a spiral, leaving a one inch loop at the top and a one inch space in the spiral after 5 inches. Continue for 9 inches more. Tie a loop in the ends and loop in a 7 inch tassel. Make a 2nd hanging cord in the same way.

44 Circular pillow cover

You will need
2 4oz skeins rug wool
Pillow form 16in in diameter
½yd lining material

Measurements
Diameter, 16in

How to make the pillow cover
Make cover for pillow form.
Cut 10 lengths each 66 inches, 10 lengths each

43 inches, 30 lengths each 40 inches and 10 lengths each 18 inches.
Cut a foundation thread of 6 inches. Double 9 of the 66 inch lengths and attach them onto the foundation thread. Push the knots together closely and tie the foundation thread tightly in a ring. Cut off the ends. Set the 10th doubled thread over the knot. Pin the ring to the center of the pillow. Divide the threads into groups of 4 and make one square knot on each group in a ring around the center. Make 2 more rings of 5 alternating square knots and make 2 more square knots directly underneath the last ring of knots.
Attach 2 doubled 43 inch lengths onto each square knot on the 2nd ring positioning the knot to the back of the work. Make 3 square knots on each of these 5 groups.
Make a ring of 10 alternating square knots. Make one square knot under each square knot.
Attach 10 doubled 40 inch lengths onto each of the last 10 square knots positioning the knot to the back of the work. There are now 6 threads in each group.
Using the 3rd thread as a leader, DHH diagonally to the left with threads 2 and 1. Knot another row of diagonal DHHs directly underneath. Using the 4th thread as a leader, DHH diagonally to the right with threads 5 and 6. Knot another row of diagonal DHHs directly underneath. Join the last 2 threads in each group to the first 2 of the adjacent group and make a square knot.
Double 2 of the 40 inch lengths and pin the doubled ends about ½ inch below the center of each group of DHHs. Make a square knot, using the 2 center threads as a core, tying it directly under the loops.
Using the first thread in the new group as a leader, DHH diagonally to the left with the 3 adjacent threads from the group directly above. Knot another row of diagonal DHHs directly underneath. Using the 3rd thread in the new group as a leader, DHH diagonally to the right with the 3 adjacent threads from the group above. Knot another row of diagonal DHH directly underneath. Make a square knot with the 6 threads in the middle of each group using the 4 center threads as a core.
Make a square knot with the first and the last 2 threads in each adjacent group. Take these threads and using the 2nd as a leader, DHH diagonally to the left with the next 4 threads. Knot another row of diagonal DHHs to the left directly underneath. Using the 3rd thread from the square knot as a leader, DHH diagonally to the right with the next 4 threads. Knot another row of diagonal DHHs to the right directly underneath. Link the DHHs with a square knot. Attach one thread doubled onto each of the square knots marked by * to *.
Take this doubled thread and the adjacent thread on either side and make a square knot. Make 3 rows of alternating square knots all the way around the pillow.

To finish
Divide threads into groups of 8 and tie together in a collecting knot (see diagram on page 94). Cut ends evenly in a tassel.
Sew macramé in place with small stitches at each collecting knot.

45 Curtain fringe

You will need
Seine twine or Lilyfine nylon macramé cord
(70yds for every 12in of fringe)

Measurements
Depth, 8in
Fringe, 7in

How to make the curtain fringe
The fringe is worked in patterns of 12 threads, each pattern measuring 2 inches across. Cut 34 lengths for every 12 inches of fringe each 72 inches and 8 lengths each about 4 inches longer than the finished fringe, one to act as foundation thread and 7 to act as horizontal DHH leaders.
Attach the required number of lengths onto the foundation thread. Using separate leader, knot one row horizontal DHHs.
Divide the threads into groups of 4 and make 2 double knotted chain on each group.
Knot 2 rows of horizontal DHHs, each time introducing a leader.
Divide the threads into groups of 12 and * on each group make the top half of a double diagonal cross. Using both pairs of outside threads make 3 knotted chain and on the next pairs of threads make one knotted chain.
Complete the double diagonal cross*.
Cross the leaders of adjoining groups.
Divide the threads into groups of 2 and with the 2nd and 5th groups, counting from the left, make one knotted chain and with the center 2 groups make 2 knotted chain.
Divide threads into groups of 12 and repeat from * to *
Knot 2 rows of horizontal DHHs.
Repeat from ** to **.
Knot another 2 rows of horizontal DHHs. Divide the threads into groups of 4 and make an overhand knot on each group.

To finish
Trim the tassels to 7 inches and tease out the thread to form a fringe.
Sew in ends of foundation thread and leaders.

46 Firescreen

You will need
300yds thick cotton twine
(White seine twine may be dyed to desired color.)
Wrought iron firescreen frame
Lining
Glue

Measurements
Height of screen, 30in
Macramé rectangle 24in by 19in

How to make the screen
Make skeins of thread and dye to the color of your choice.
Cut 2 lengths each 60 inches, 2 lengths each 192 inches and 62 lengths each 165 inches. Attach the 60 inch lengths one on each side of the screen, so that they run from the top to the bottom of the screen.

Detail of a corner of the firescreen. Notice how the threads are wrapped over the edge thread

DHH the ends of the threads to the bottom bar of the screen. These lengths serve to secure the rest of the work. They are not actually incorporated into the working.
Double the 2 192 inch lengths and attach them on at each end within the edge threads. Double the 165 inch lengths and attach them on in between.
First row
Leaving out the edge threads, make a square knot with the first 4 threads.
Leave 6 threads and with the next 8 threads make one double knotted chain. Leave 6 threads and make a square knot on the next 4 threads. Repeat from * to * until the end of the row.
2nd row
Starting at the left, make a square knot on threads 3, 4, 5 and 6. Make a square knot on threads 5, 6, 7 and 8. Continue working square knots in a sloping line in to the right. Each square knot should consist of 2 threads from the previous square knot and the 2 adjoining threads. Work until there are 6 square knots.
To make the 4 diamonds across the screen start at the square knots worked between the knotted chain. These are the apexes of the 4 diamonds **Take 2 threads from the left of the square knot and the next 2 threads and make a square knot. Continue in this way to make a sloping line of square knots to the left until there are 6 square knots. Repeat this to the right. **Repeat from ** to ** across the row and at the end make the half-pattern as for the half-pattern at the beginning of the row.
Make a square knot between each square knot pattern, making a 7th square knot common to both patterns. From this point the square knots slope back again.
3rd row
Having worked the outlines of the diamond pattern across the work, now fill the diamonds with square knots. With the full-size diamonds, take the 4 center threads and make a square knot. The left half of this square knot starts a series of square knots to the left, and the right half to the right. The rows will consist of 6, 5, 4, 3, 2 and one square knot counting from the center.
At the sides, wrap the 2 threads next to the edge thread over the latter and back underneath through the loop thus formed (see page 99). These 2 threads plus the next 2 along from the center square knot in the half diamond pattern on the edge. In each row the 2 threads next to the edge thread are wrapped around it as described. When the square knot diamonds are complete, there will be 4 complete shapes and 2 half-patterns at the side.
The knotted chain patterns
These occur in the spaces between the square knot diamonds.
Take the center threads hanging from the diamonds and make one knotted chain.
With the 4 threads on the left of this knot plus the next 4 hanging threads, make one double knotted chain. Repeat this on the right. Take the 8 center threads and make one double knotted chain. Adjust knots so that they lie in a square in relation to each other and equidistant from the edges of the square knot diamonds.
Knot these 2 patterns alternately until there are 8 square knot diamonds in the vertical pattern. Make one double knotted chain in the half-patterns between them as in the first row.
To finish
Fasten the loose threads to the frame with DHH knots except for the 8 threads hanging from each of the knotted chain groups. These are arranged 4 on each side of the frame and knotted underneath the bottom bar in pairs with an overhand knot. Knot all the other threads underneath in pairs with an overhand knot, cut ends and coat thickly with clear glue.

A lining can be sewn loosely into the back of the macramé rectangle so that the knots can be seen more clearly.
N.B. This screen should never be stood in front of a lighted fire. It is designed purely for decorative purposes.

47 Lampshade

You will need
2 balls polypropylene twine
One 5in lampshade ring with light fitting
One 6in ring
One 7in ring
32 ½in diameter rings

Measurements
7in wide at widest part
10in deep including fringe

To make a lampshade
Cut 38 threads each 80 inches. Attach 19 sets of 2 doubled threads, each with 2 picots and one square knot before being knotted onto first 5 inch ring. Make one round of square knots. Slot the left hand thread of each knot and the right hand thread of the knot directly to the left through the same ring all the way around and then work another row of square knots. Make one row of alternating square knots. Using a separate thread. make one row horizontal DHH, darning in ends afterwards. Using the same grouping in fours as on previous row of square knots, work 8 square knots on each group. Knot one row horizontal DHHs onto 7 inch ring. Divide the threads into alternate groups of 4 and make a further 8 square knots. Knot a row of horizontal DHHs over the 6 inch ring. Make one row square knots, link groups with rings as before and make another row of square knots. Make one row alternate square knots. Using separate length of thread, knot 2 rows horizontal DHHs.
To finish
Darn in the ends of the separate thread and even remaining thread to make fringe. Fray.

48 Waste paper basket

You will need
300yds cotton seine twine
Waste paper basket
Material to cover basket
Glue

Measurements
Depth, 10½in
Width, 8½in x 6½in
Circumference, 24in

How to cover the basket with material
Measure around the basket and cut out the material to fit, allowing a few inches for the join. Dab glue at the top and bottom of the basket leaving the rim free. Glue material to the basket and allow to dry.

How to make the waste paper basket cover
Cut 76 lengths each 96 inches. (If you are working on a basket of a different circumference remember that the total number of knotting

threads must be divisible by 8.) Cut one length long enough to go around the basket plus a few more inches, and mount onto working surface.
Take 2 lengths and tie an overhand knot in the center of these lengths. Double them over and DHH onto the foundation thread, so that the overhand knot is at the top of this thread. Repeat from * to * until all lengths have been mounted. Dab glue around the top of the basket (now covered with material), take the foundation threads from working surface, tie firmly around the basket and allow to dry.
Divide threads into groups of 8 so that the leaf pattern can be worked. **Using thread 8 as a leader DHH to the left with threads 1 to 7 curving slightly downward as you work. To complete the leaf shape, take the thread farthest on the right, and using it as a leader, DHH to the left, curving slightly upward. Repeat from ** to ** all the way around the basket.
Counting to the right in each group of 8, take thread 5 as a leader and DHH to the right with the last 3 threads and continue DHHs into the next group with the first 4 threads, curving it downward. Complete the lower half of the leaf using the same threads. Repeat from*** to*** all the way around the basket. Cut one length long enough to go around the basket plus a few more inches. Tie it loosely around the basket over the knotting threads, directly underneath the leaf pattern. Knot one row of horizontal DHHs, using all the threads. When you have completed this row, untie the first DHH knot worked and pull up the excess thread. Tie it to fit closely around the basket.
Divide the total number of threads in half and tie the other half out of the way, so that the work is being done on only one side of the basket. Take the 4 center threads and make a square knot. Make 2 square knots on either side of this one with the next 8 threads. Underneath these 5 square knots make 4 rows of alternating square knots, discontinuing 2 threads on either side at each row, so that the number of square knots reduce. The knots should go down to form a point with only one square knot on the last row. Take the next free thread on the right and nearest the first row of 5 square knots, and using it as a leader DHH diagonally to the left with the 10 adjacent threads.
Knot another row of diagonal DHHs to the left using the next free thread on the top right as a leader. Repeat double diagonal DHHs on the left working in to the right. Make a square knot with the 4 center threads, so that the rows of DHHs are joined together. Take the 2 threads on either side of this square knot and knot 3 more square knots with these threads, using the 4 threads from the first square knot as a core. Make one more square knot with the 4 center threads only. Leave these 8 threads hanging.
On the right of the work there are 8 threads hanging from the 2nd row of diagonal DHHs. Using the first of these threads on the left as a leader, DHH diagonally upward to the right with the remaining 7 threads, and then continue the row of DHHs with the next 3 free threads on the right, so that 10 threads in all have been used for the DHH, plus one thread for the leader. See angle of DHHs in photograph on page opposite, Leave the leader hanging to be used later. Make another row of DHHs to the right and directly underneath the first row, using the first thread as a leader. DHH over the next 9 threads. Using the same thread as a leader, DHH back from right to left with threads 9 to one. Then, using the leader left hanging from the first row of DHHs, take it around the right hand end of the last 2 rows of DHHs, and work back from right to left with threads 10 to one. This completes the first petal shape.
The next shape is worked so that it touches the first one at the inner edge. Use the first thread as a

Detail from waste paper basket

leader and DHH horizontally to the left with the next 10 threads. Continue making the 2nd petal shape like the first.

Make the 3rd petal shape like the 2nd but DHH diagonally downward to the right.

Return to the left hand side of the work and repeat the motifs described above, making sure that the petal shapes correspond with those on the right. Having finished the motifs, knot double diagonal DHHs to left and right and 5 rows of alternating square knots to correspond with the pattern described previously, (see photograph on page 101). Leave 5 threads on either side of the center motif and make approximately 11 double alternating knotted chains on the next 4 threads directly along to right and left. Leave the next 4 threads and make double knotted chain on the next 4. Continue to knot the areas in between the 2 center motifs in this way.

When this is completed, knot a row of horizontal DHHs, 2 rows of leaf shapes and another row of horizontal DHHs to correspond with those at the top of the basket.

Complete the other side of the basket in the same way as described above.

To finish

Turn basket upside down. Run a line of glue all around its lower rim. Take a few threads from one side of the work and tie them firmly with the threads from the other side of the work, knotting them across the base of the basket. Continue in this way until all the threads are knotted, so as to stretch the work downward. Leave to dry. Untie the knots at the base of the basket and make overhand knots on each group of 4 threads. Cut off the excess threads. Add a little glue to keep the cut ends in place.

49 Placemat and napkin ring

You will need
96yds Lilyfine nylon macramé cord
One inch plastic curtain ring

Measurements
Mat. Center to point of star, approximately 7in including fringe
Napkin ring. 7in by 2in

How to make the mat
Cut 25 lengths each 60 inches, 10 lengths each 50 inches, 20 lengths each 36 inches and 5 lengths each 30 inches.

Attach 15 of the 65 inch lengths onto the ring.
*Group 4 threads and make one square knot, skip 2 threads, repeat from * all around.

Use each group of 2 threads not yet knotted as cores, and one thread on either side from the square knots already made to make 2 square knots all around. In each of the 10 spaces between the first and 2nd sets of square knots set on another 60 inch length with the knot facing the back of the work (see diagram a).

Using the 2 center threads from the first set of square knots as leaders, lay them to right and left respectively and knot diagonal DHHs across 2 threads just attached and 2 from the 2nd set of square knots. Repeat this all around so that 10 DHHs are formed.

Using the first thread from the DHHs just worked as leader, knot a 2nd row of diagonal DHHs across next 4 threads. Extend this DHH row by attaching on a 50 inch thread to the leader with the knot to the back as before. Continue the DHHs across these 2 additional threads. Repeat in this way all around. Join each adjacent set of DHHs by DHH knotting the leader from the left onto the right-hand leader. Using the 4 threads from each of the inner points of the star, make 2 square knots.

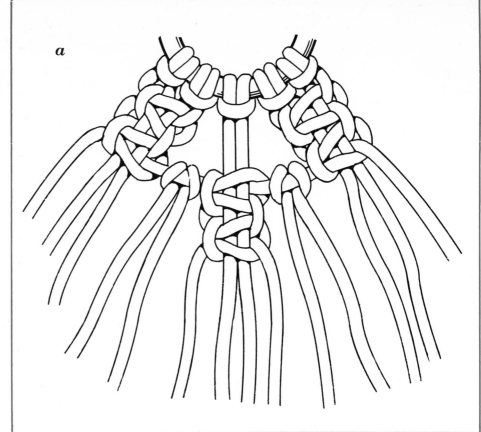

a

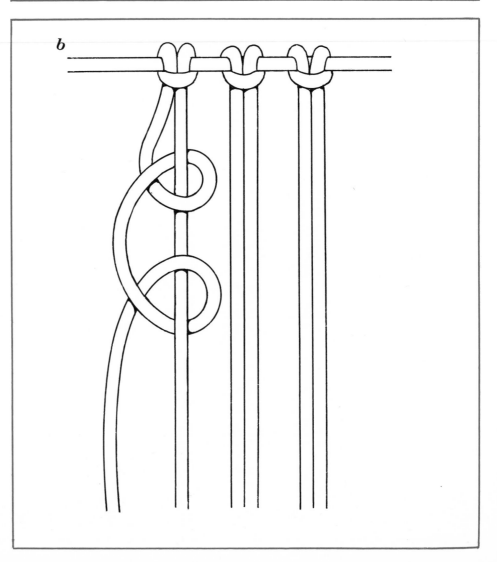

b

Take the 2 center threads from these square knots and lay them to the left and right respectively. These threads should lie approximately one inch from the previous DHHs. Using these threads as leaders, knot diagonal DHHs across the next 6 threads. Extend this DHH row by attaching 2 36 inch threads to the leader with the knot to the back as before. Continue the DHHs across these 4 additional threads. Join the points of the star by pinning a 30 inch thread doubled at each point. DHH one end onto the leader on the left and the other end onto the right-hand leader. Pull this up tightly to close the gap.

With the 4 threads at each point, make one square knot.

Using the 4 threads from each of the inner points of the star, make a square knot. Continue making square knots down each side of the DHHs, all around. Make 3 rows of alternating square knots all around.

To finish

Divide the threads into groups of 2 threads from each square knot and make an overhand knot on each group, making 60 knots in all.

Trim the fringe as required.

How to make the napkin ring

Cut 6 lengths each 70 inches.

Pin one doubled thread to the working surface with 2 pins placed 2 inches apart in the center of the thread so that an inverted U is formed (see photograph), the base to be used as a foundation thread. Pin the center of a 2nd thread one inch above the center of the thread already pinned. DHH each end of the foundation thread.

On each side of these center threads attach 2 more threads.

Using the 2nd thread in as leader, knot a vertical DHH with the outer thread on each side, taking the thread to the back of the work (see diagram b). Divide the remaining 8 threads into groups of 4 and make one square knot on each group, using 2 threads as core.

Take the inner 2 threads from each sqaure knot to form an alternated group and make one square knot. *Leave the outer thread on each side free. Using the 2nd threads as leaders, DHH diagonally into the center over next 4 threads.

Using the 2nd thread in on each side as leader, knot 4 vertical DHHs as before with the outside threads.

Continue the diagonal DHHs to form a cross.

Using 4 center threads, make a square knot with 2 threads as core.

Using the 2 outer threads from this knot and the 2 threads on either side, make 2 square knots alternated with the first.

Make 3 more square knots alternated with the previous 2 square knots.

Make 3 more square knots under the center one and form these 4 square knots into a blackberry ball. Secure with one square knot. Make one square knot on either side of this center square knot.

Make 2 square knots alternated with the previous 3 square knots.

Use the 4 center threads to make a square knot.* Repeat from * to *.

Leave the outer threads on each side free. Using the 2nd threads as leaders, DHH diagonally into center over next 4 threads. Join the V shape in the middle by DHH knotting the left leader onto the right leader. Knot 4 vertical DHHs as before down each side.

Make a blackberry ball as before and secure with one square knot.

Make 2 square knots alternated with the previous square knot and then 3 alternated square knots.

To finish

Turn the free ends under and sew in neatly.

Fasten top loop over last blackberry ball.

Napkin ring

50 Hassock

You will need

3 2oz skeins each of orange, beige, pink in rug wool
2 2oz skeins each of red, brown in rug wool
Circle of suede or leather, 14in diameter
6 suede or leather strips ½in by 14in
Length of cane or cord 48in

Measurements

Depth, 9in
Diameter, 14in

How to make the hassock

Mark 6 equally spaced points around the circle of suede or leather and punch 28 holes between each pair of marks at ¼ inch intervals, ½ inch in from edge, 168 holes altogether.
Punch one hole in each end of the leather strips.
Cut 20 lengths each 96 inches in orange, beige and pink. Cut 12 lengths each 96 inches in red and brown.

Attach lengths double through the holes in the leather in the following order: *2 brown, 2 red, (2 orange, 2 beige) twice, (one orange, 2 beige) twice, 2 orange, 2 beige, 2 orange, 2 red, 2 brown threading the right-hand thread of the 2nd doubled brown lengths through the end of a leather strip as well as the hole in the circle, repeat from * substituting pink for orange, then repeat from * again, this time returning to orange as for the first section and substituting pink for the beige. Repeat from * again this time as for the first section but reversing the beige and orange. Repeat from * again this time as for the 2nd section but reversing the pink and beige. Repeat from * finally as for 3rd section but reversing the orange and pink.
Lay cane or cord over the holes overlapping the ends and thinning them to keep an even thickness use as leader to DHH each thread over it to secure. Pin the work to the top of the hassock. Starting at the beginning of the first section, divide the thread into groups of 4 and make one square knot on each group except the center group of each section. On each center group use the 2 center cords as core and make the first half of a square knot 4 times with the outer 2 threads to make a spiral. On the next row alternate the groupings so that between the sections the leather strip, as well as the 2 center threads, are used as a core for the

square knot and make a spiral as before on the 2 center groups of each section.
Continue in this way for 3 more rows, alternating the groupings and increasing by one more spiral on each row.
Continue for 3 more rows alternating the groups at each leather strip, making either one square knot on the strip or one at each side of it. After the first of these rows leave the outer thread at each side free and make the 2 square knots on the next row with only one core thread, at the same time decreasing by one spiral on each row and leaving the remaining threads to hang free.
Continue on the spirals section until only one spiral is worked. Then, using the thread left free from the square knots as leader, DHH diagonally down the side of the spirals section across all threads. On the next row of alternated square knots at each leather strip, take the 2 center threads behind the strip, using the first 2 threads from the diagonal DHHs as a core, make a square knot around them with 2 threads from the square knots and the next 2 threads from the diagonal DHHs.
Continue working alternating square knots in the usual way down the leather strips. Knot the leaders of the diagonal DHHs at the point where they meet and then continue diagonal DHHs to right and left across all threads except outer 2 threads at each side of each section.
Using the center 2 threads of each section as core, make a square knot around them with the 2 threads on either side.
Using the 6th thread out from the center at each side as leader, knot diagonal DHHs into the center of each section and cross leaders.
Counting out from the center again, use the 5th to 10th threads inclusive to make a square knot with with a 2 thread core.
Make a square knot over each leather strip.
Continue the center cross of diagonal DHHs to half way across the threads of both square knots, and using the leader from the larger diagonal DHH, cross the cord back in to meet the smaller cross under the square knot. Cross one leader over the other. Make a square knot on the center 6 threads of each section and a square knot with the 6 threads on either side of each leather strip.

To finish

Using a separate length of about 24 inches to make a circle in the center of the hassock base and taking the threads in pairs, knot each pair in an overhand knot around this thread.
Trim and glue ends lightly to the base of the hassock. Glue ends of leather strips to base of hassock under threads.

Crash Course
in
Macramé

The only tools needed for macramé are threads, a knotting board and a pair of hands. Here is the basic know-how for this fascinating craft.

Attaching threads

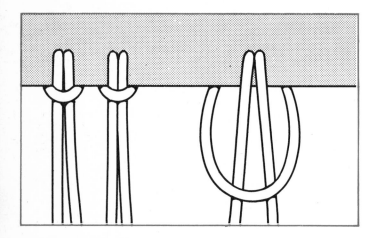

To knot onto fabric
Threads must be about eight times the length of the finished work and then folded in half to form doubled threads. Pull the doubled thread through the material with a crochet hook and knot the ends through the loop. Pull the knot firmly up to the edge of the fabric but not so tightly that the fabric puckers.

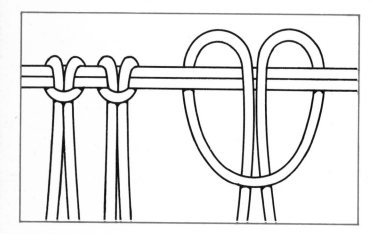

To knot separately
Cut a length of yarn about six inches longer than the finished width of the work. Pin to the top of knotting board with overhand knots so that it is taut and running under the attached knots.
Cut working threads eight times the length of the finished work. Fold each thread in half and tie onto the foundation thread by holding the doubled strand in front of the foundation thread, fold it over the back and pull the ends through the loop, tightening the knot around the foundation thread. Having the doubled threads four times the length of the finished work is only a guide. The thicker the thread is, the more length will be used up by each knot.
The attached threads are pushed close together and it helps to prevent tangling if each thread is wound into a small ball secured with a rubber band. The thread can then be fed out as it is required.

Horizontal double half hitches (DHH)

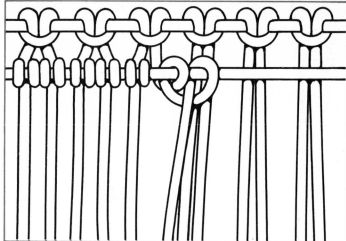

The attached threads are usually secured with one row of horizontal DHHs. The double half hitch (DHH) is the basic knot of all macramé. Each knot is worked over a leader and this can either be a second foundation thread introduced from the side of the work or an outer edge thread. A separate thread should be six inches longer than the finished width of the work, the same as the first foundation thread. The leader is held taut by the right hand, running horizontally below the attached knots and on top of the knotting threads.

Working from left to right, bring up each single knotting thread in turn and knot it around the knot bearer to form a knot. Repeat the same movement a second time to form the double half hitch.
Pull the knot tight and repeat these two steps with the next thread.
As well as making a firm base for beginning or finishing a piece of macramé, horizontal DHHs can be used within the design but always using one of the knotting threads as leader and not a separate foundation thread.

Double horizontal double half hitches

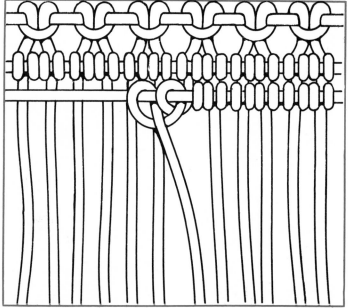

Introduce a third foundation thread or use the outer edge thread and knot another line of DHHs from right to left. The knots will be worked in the same way as explained above but the thread will be knotted around clockwise as opposed to counter-clockwise.

Diagonal double half hitches (stage 1)

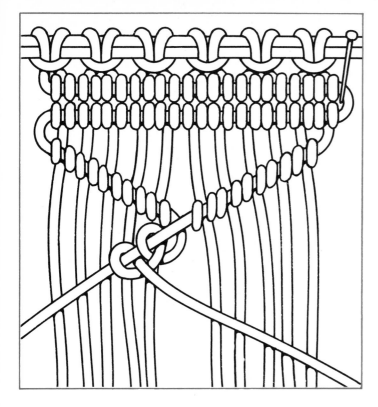

Double diagonal DHHs (stage 1)

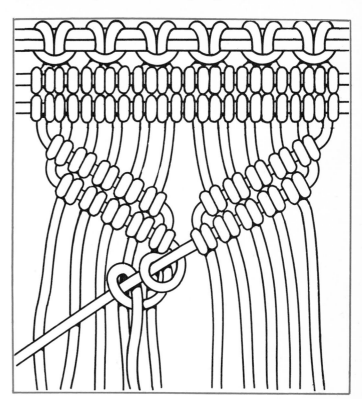

This is worked in the same way as the horizontal DHH, using one of the knotting threads as a leader, which is held diagonally downward to either right or left, depending on which way the work is intended to slope and over the threads to be knotted.

The thread next to the leader is knotted around it in the same knot as for the horizontal DHH. Continue along the row until a diagonal bar of double half hitches is formed. Cross leaders in the middle as shown in diagram stage 2.

Work one row of diagonal double half hitches on the right and left using the first and last thread as a leader. Take the outside threads and knot another row of diagonal DHHs. parallel to the rows already knotted.

DHH the leader on the right across to the left. DHH the next thread in the section on the left, across to the left. Complete the cross by DHH knotting the leader on the left across to the right. DHH the next thread in the section on the right, across to the right.

Diagonal double half hitches (stage 2)

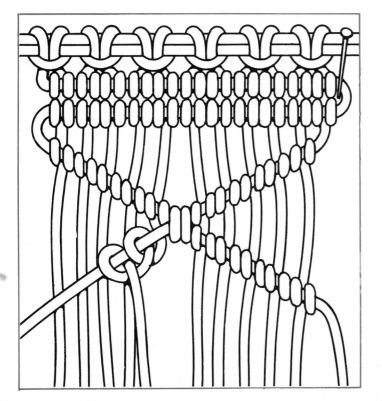

Double diagonal DHHs (stage 2)

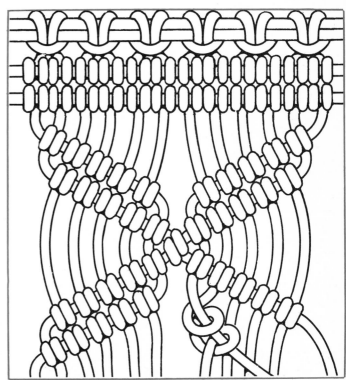

Square knots

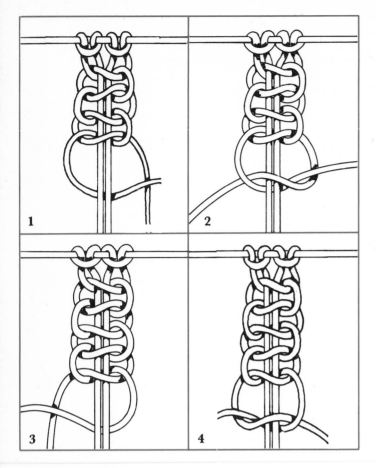

Alternating square knots

Attach knots in multiples of four. Make a square knot in each group.

In the next row skip two threads and with the next four threads make a square knot. Make another square knot with the next four and so on until the end of the row. Two threads will remain on either side. These will then be incorporated into the work onthe next row.

Continue knotting the rows in this way so that each knot is formed alternately.

The square knot is the second basic knot of macramé.

To make square knots, four threads, or multiples of four, are required. The two center threads act as a core and the two outer threads are knotted around them. Hold the center threads taut by winding them around the third finger of the left hand or by securing them to the bottom of the board with a bulldog clip.

Form the right-hand thread into a loop with the end passing under the center core and over the left-hand thread. Bring the left-hand thread over the core and thread it through the loop from the front of the work.

Pull both ends up until the knot closes tightly around the center core. This completes the first part of the knot.

Repeat the process in reverse by forming the left-hand thread into a loop and passing the right-hand thread through the loop. Draw up tight. If only one half of the square knot is repeated continuously the resulting braid

will spiral. The direction of the spiral depends on whether the first or second step is used.

Finishing

Turn back the threads and sew them down at the back of the fabric for about a quarter of an inch, then trim the ends closely. Do the same with the foundation thread. This method is more practical for macramé than darning in the ends as for knitting or crochet because the tightness of the knots makes too firm a fabric to work into. If there is any likelihood of the yarn fraying allow a slightly longer end.

Adding more threads

If the thread is used up before the work is completed, add an extra length by overcasting one end to the end already incorporated in the work. The threads could also be knotted together providing the knot falls to the back of the work.

Double half hitch diamond and a square knot

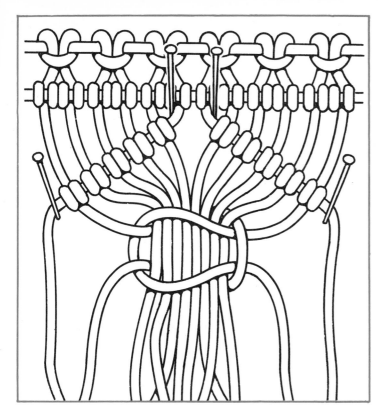

Knot the center threads with DHHs out to the left and right diagonally (see diagonal DHH page 107)

Temporarily leave both leaders on either side and make a square knot with the center threads. In the diagram eight threads have been used as a core and two threads used for knotting around them.

Insert a pin just inside each outside leader thread, and double half hitch over the leaders diagonally towards the center.

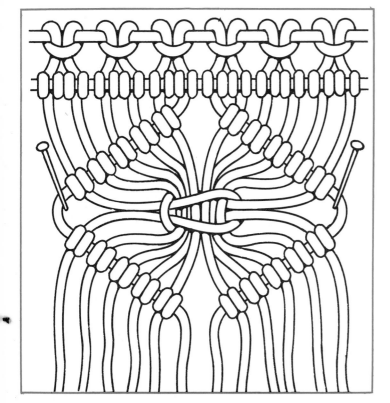

Square knots with picots

Attach two doubled threads and make one square knot. Make a second square knot leaving a space between it and the first one. Push the knot up into place under the first one. The length of thread left between the two knots dictates the size of the picot.

Square knots with side knots

Attach doubled threads and make a square knot. Tie an overhand knot (see page 110) on each of the right and left threads using a pin to slide the knots up against the preceding square knot before finally tightening it. Make a second square knot.

Square knots with beads

Attach two doubled threads and make one square knot. Thread a bead onto each of the left and right-hand threads and make a second square knot.

N.B. Choose beads which have large holes so that they are easily threaded.

Children's china or wooden threading beads, and small rings available for various purposes from notions departments all add an attractive three-dimensional look to macramé.

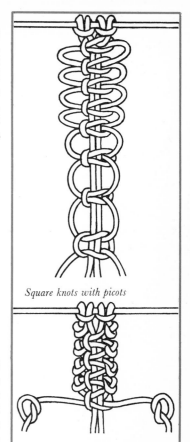

Square knots with picots

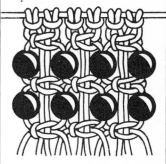

Square knots with side knots

Square knots with beads

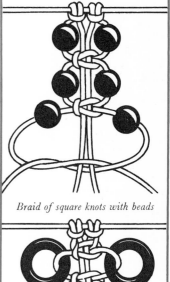

Braid of square knots with beads

Overhand knot

An overhand knot can be made with any number of threads. All thicknesses are held together and used as one to form a loop into which the working end is inserted, top to bottom and front to back. The ends are then pulled to tighten the knot.

Making an overhand knot

Blackberry balls

This decorative bobble is usually made over four threads. Make six square knots, then using a blunt ended needle, thread the two center threads from front to

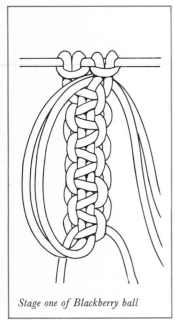

Stage one of Blackberry ball

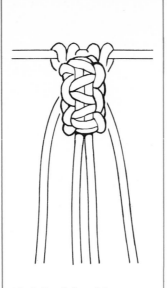

The ball pulled up tight

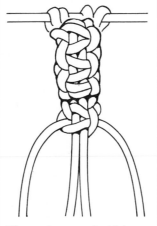

The securing square knot below

back through the work above the center of the first knot. Pull up until a little blackberry-shaped roll is formed. The next square knot which is made underneath this will then hold the blackberry ball in place.

Picots and scallops

Attaching threads on a foundation cord can be done in more decorative ways than simple knotting by using picots or scallops.

Simple picots. Pin doubled threads behind the foundation cord. Attach to the cord with DHHs.

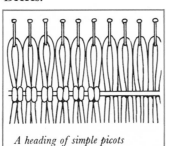

A heading of simple picots

Scallops. Pin doubled threads as for simple picots but using three threads, one inside the other. Keep the spacing even by pinning. DHH to the foundation.

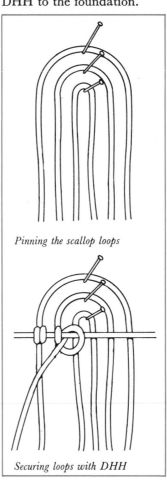

Pinning the scallop loops

Securing loops with DHH

Knotted picots. Place three doubled threads side by side behind the foundation cord with the center thread slightly higher than those on either

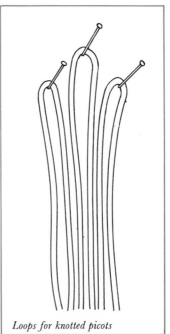

Loops for knotted picots

side. Make a square knot using the four center threads as a core. Knot with a row of horizontal DHHs to foundation cord.

Knotted scallops. Pin two doubled threads, one inside the other. Make two square knots and attach scallops to foundation cord with DHHs.

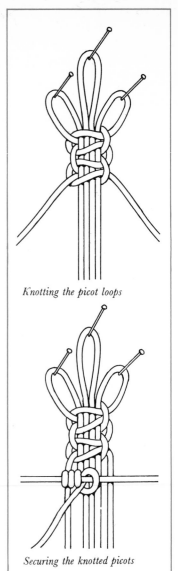

Knotting the picot loops

Securing the knotted picots

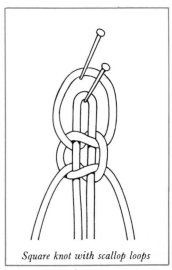

Square knot with scallop loops

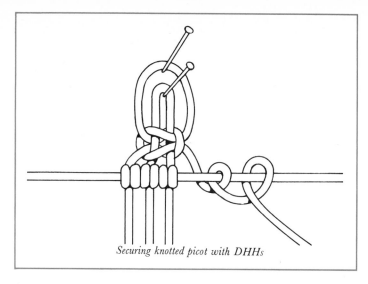

Securing knotted picot with DHHs

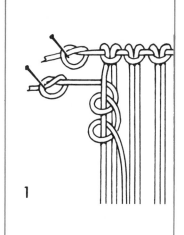

1

Joining in the pattern thread with a vertical DHH

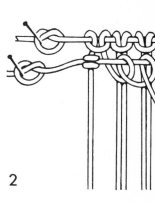

2

Using the pattern thread as horizontal DHH leader

Knotted chain

Chains are made by alternating single half hitches from left to right. A left and right hand knot make one knotted chain.

Knotting thread left

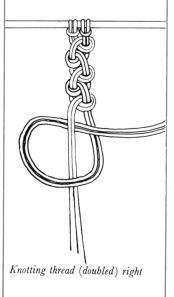

Knotting thread (doubled) right

Cavandoli

In this technique only two colors and one knot are used. Traditionally, the horizontal. DHHs provide the background and the vertical DHHs form the pattern. The result is a smooth, tightly knotted fabric.

The horizontal DHHs are horizontal DHHs as given in the previous part of the macramé crash course.

The vertical DHH knot is exactly the same but the hanging thread is used as leader and a second thread is knotted down the length of this leader. The knotting thread always starts by passing behind the leader so that when travelling across the work to the right the knots face to the right, and when returning across the work on the next row the knots point to the left.

The threads in the background color are attached on the foundation thread, and the ball of thread in the pattern color is attached to the left hand corner of the work, from where it is used as a leader for the horizontal DHHs or used to make the vertical DHH knots which form the pattern.

Designs are worked out on squared paper using crosses for pattern and blank squares for background. The resulting work, however, is elongated in comparison to the square shape of the original chart.

It is traditional to knot the first and last threads in vertical DHHs with a little picot

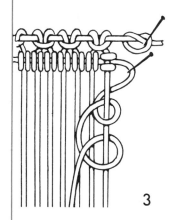

3

Pinning thread for picot: making first vertical DHH

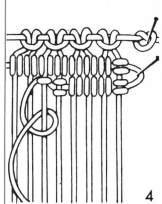

4

Knotting the pattern in vertical DHHs as required

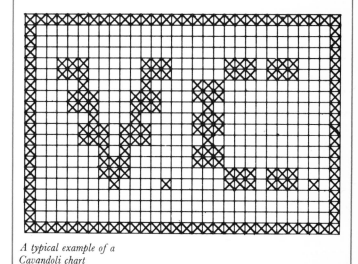

A typical example of a Cavandoli chart

when the thread is turned, thus forming a pretty border. Allow at least eight times the length of the finished article for the background color threads. The pattern color is all in one ball and is the same length as the total of all the background threads added together. Roll each thread into a ball to prevent tangling.